Talk Time

Everyday English Conversation

Student Book 1

Susan Stempleski

OXFORD
UNIVERSITY PRESS

OXFORD
UNIVERSITY PRESS

...dison Avenue
...ork, NY 10016 USA

...eat Clarendon Street, Oxford OX2 6DP UK

Oxford University Press is a department of the University of Oxford.
It furthers the University's objective of excellence in research, scholarship,
and education by publishing worldwide in

Oxford   New York
Auckland Cape Town Dar es Salaam Hong Kong Karachi
Kuala Lumpur Madrid Melbourne Mexico City Nairobi
New Delhi Shanghai Taipei Toronto

With offices in
Argentina Austria Brazil Chile Czech Republic France Greece
Guatemala Hungary Italy Japan Poland Portugal Singapore
South Korea Switzerland Thailand Turkey Ukraine Vietnam

OXFORD and OXFORD ENGLISH are registered trademarks of
Oxford University Press.

© Oxford University Press 2007

Database right Oxford University Press (maker)

Library of Congress Cataloging-In-Publication Data

Stempleski, Susan.
     Talk time: student book / Susan Stempleski.
       p. cm.
     Contents: — [1] Book 1 — [2] Book 2 — [3] Book 3.
     ISBN 978-0-19-438201-4 (Student bk. 1)
     ISBN 978-0-19-438208-3 (Student bk. 2)
     ISBN 978-0-19-438217-5 (Student bk. 3)
     1. English language—Textbooks for foreign speakers.
     2. English language—Grammar—Problems, exercises, etc. I. Title

PE1128.S743 2006
428.2'4—dc22

                                        2006040020

Market Development Director, Asia: Chris Balderston
Senior Editor: Patricia O'Neill
Art Director: Maj-Britt Hagsted
Senior Designer: Stacy Merlin
Art Editor: Elizabeth Blomster
Production Manager: Shanta Persaud
Production Controller: Eve Wong

ISBN 978 0 19 439289 1 (Student Book with CD)
ISBN 978 0 19 438201 4 (Student Book)

Printed in Hong Kong

10 9 8 7 6 5

ACKNOWLEDGMENTS

Illustrations by: Dwight Allot/Three In A Box Inc. pp.1, 17(objects), 39; Mark Collins/
Deborah Wolfe ltd. pp. 14, 27, 35(rooms); Richard Deverell pp.18, 24, 31(house
cutaway top), 36, 73, 75; Rob Kemp/Deborah Wolfe Ltd. pp.3, 9, 53, 60, 66. 76;
Janos Jatner/Beehive Illustration pp. 7, 10, 16, 17(people pointing), 55; Katie
Mac/NB Illustration Ltd. pp.5, 8, 20, 56, 65; Marc Monés/American Artists pp. 29,
35(man looking for cell phone), 62, 71; Leif Peng pp. 23(person sleeping, reading
and eating), 28, 64; Pulsar Studio/Beehive Illustration pp. 23(people on phone),
30, 42, 52; Marco Schaaf/NB Illustration Ltd. pp. 17(salesman), 23(people in cities),
61, 67; Rob Schuster pp. 51, 72; William Waitzman pp. 12, 13, 31(house floor
plan bottom), 47, 69; Lawrence Whiteley/NB Illustration Ltd. pp.49; Tracey Wood/
Reactor Art & Design pp. 6, 21, 50, 57, 74

Location and Studio Photography by:
Dennis Kitchen Studio pp. 14, 15, 57

We would like to thank the following for their permission to reproduce photographs:
Alamy: Ace Stock Limited, 5(Australian female); Banana Stock, 53(men watching
TV), 80(dog); Blend Images, 5(Chinese male), 80(woman reading newspaper);
Brand X Pictures, 5(Korean female); Comstock Premium, 25(soda); Cut and Dealt
Ltd., 72(basketball game); Digital Archive Japan, 5(Japanese man), 43(holding
hands); Image 100, 43(present), 46(relaxing); ImageState, 80(man on scooter);
Judith Collins, 28(popcorn);Mylife photos,70(laundry); Nick Emm, 16(digital
camera); Peter Horree, 64(Hong Kong shopping); Photodisc, 72(theater),
82(balcony); Purestock, 80(shopping); Scott Hortop, 64(moving in); Stock
Connection Distribution, 22(teen on cell); Stockdisc Classic, 28(rice cakes);
Thinkstock, 82(stairs); Warren Diggles, 5(American male and female); Corbis:
Royalty-Free,2(outdoor party), 34(dresser), 58(bath); Keith Dannemill/Nikon D-
100, 43(uniforms); David Madison/zefa, 40(volleyball); Comstock: Jupiter Images
Unlimited, 68(female on phone); Getty: Beateworks, 82(bathroom); Blend Images,
72(restaurant); Nick Dolfing, 70(female studying); Bob Elsdale, 40(judo); John
Glustina, 26(students outdoors); William Howard, 22(reading email); Jeff Kaufman,
59(female doctor); James Levin, 43(Mom and child); Ryan McVay, 5(Indian female);
Megan Maloy, 19(shower); Eri Morita, 72(shopping); Steve Neidorf Photography,
70(going to bed); Chris Nobel, 42(hiking); Mike Powell, 40(soccer);Andy Sacks,
64(graduation); Don Smetzer, 46(dinner); Adam Smith, 46(packing for trip); Stone,
5(British male), 82(yard); Paul Thomas, 43(engagement); Inmagine: Ablestock,
34(table); BananaStock,19(man on phone, playing piano), 28(potato chips),
37(surfing net, taking picture, café), 43(moving in, diploma), 44(chatting on
campus), 46(museum); Blend Images,19(driving, going to work), 38(cafeteria);
Brand X Pictures, 11(chatting),19(female shopping), 25(apples), 28(nuts),
37(movies), 43(baby, graduation), 70(baby-sitting); Creatas, 6(passport),16(DVD),
46(video store); Digitalvison, 22(theater, reading), 43(vacation), 46(café), 70(exam);
Comstock, 34(sofa), 41(watching TV), 43(moving); Digitalvision, 37(headphones),
58(cough syrup); Foodcollection, 25(carrots, steak), 28(pretzels); Image100,
22(shopping), 25(soup); Imageshop, 28(chocolate); Ingram, 25(tomatoes);
Photoalto, 37(playing cards), 43(party); Photodisc,5(Brazilian male), 13(eraser,
pencil, dictionary, textbook), 16(mp3 player, laptop),19(doing dishes), 25(coffee, ice
cream, pie, salad, tea), 33(big house), 34(armchair), 37(artist), 40(snowboarding),
43(handing key), 58(dentist), 72(tennis, museum); Pixtal, 28(cookies),
40(windsurfing, cycling), 46(studying), 58(sick); Stockbyte, 6(businessman),
25(cake, spaghetti), 28(fruit), 58(aspirin, jogging); Stockdisc, 13(ruler, stereo),
25(chicken, French fries), 34(bed, lamp); Thinkstock, 13(notebook), 19(studying);
Tongro, 33(country house), 34(bookcase); Punchstock; Creatas, 19(drinking
water), 82(kitchen); Image100, 33(deluxe building); Photodisc , 34(picture);
Photodisc Green, 58(drinking tea); Photodisc Red, 70(fixing bike); Stockbyte,
68(man on phone); Stockdisc, 32(women in apartment); Superstock Royalty-Free,
80(chef); Uppercut Images, 43(entering building); Uppercut Images: BananaStock,
37(watching TV), 72(beach); Digital Vision, 64(first day of school), 72(working
out); ITStock, 37(couple at beach);Image Source, 19(male sleeping), 37(shopping);
Photodisc, 19(reading email, cooking), 22(Mom cooking), 33(bungalow), 37(lifting
weights), 58(doctor), 70(listening to teacher); Photodisc Eyewire, 43(first day of
school); Stockdisc, 70(vacuuming)

*We would like to thank the following for their permission to reproduce photographs on the
cover:* Getty Images (couple); Background Images: Corbis (clock); Getty Images
(group of four teens).

The publishers would like to thank the following for their help in developing this series: Mei-ho
Chiu, Taiwan; Kirsten Duckett, Seoul, Korea; Laura MacGregor, Tokyo, Japan; Grant
Warfield, Seoul, Korea; Andrew Zitzmann, Osaka, Japan.

The publishers would also like to thank the following OUP staff for their support and assistance:
Ted Yoshioka.

Contents

Scope and sequence

Unit	Theme	Grammar	Vocabulary
1 page 1	Meeting people Countries and nationalities	*To be*; subject pronouns, possessive adjectives; Yes/No questions and short answers	Name, address, telephone number; country, nationality
2 page 7	Family Describing people	*Wh-* questions; *have*	Family relationships; adjectives: height, weight, age
3 page 13	In a classroom In an electronics store	*This / that*; preposition *on*; *these / those*; plurals	Classroom objects: book, pen, pencil; small electronics: MP3 player, laptop, cell phone
4 page 19	Everyday activities Places	Present continuous: statements, Yes/No questions; *Wh-* questions; preposition *at*	Daily activities: studying, eating, sleeping; locations and places
5 page 25	Foods and drinks Snacks	Simple present; agreeing and disagreeing; count and noncount nouns; *How much / How many*	Food and drink, meals, restaurant vocabulary; snack foods, *a lot*
6 page 31	Housing Furniture	*There is / there are*; prepositions of place	House, apartment, rooms; furniture
7 page 37	Free time activities Popular sports	Information questions; adverbs of frequency; *can* for ability	Leisure activities; sports, exercise, hobbies
8 page 43	Life events Plans for the weekend	*Be going to* future; *Wh-* questions	Life events; special occasions; weekend activities
9 page 49	Movies TV programs	*Wh-* questions; adverbs of frequency	Types of movies; types of TV programs
10 page 55	Health problems Getting better	*Feel* + adjective; *have* + noun; imperatives	Ailments, illnesses, and health; remedies
11 page 64	On vacation Past events	Simple past: questions and statements; *to be*: simple past	Vacation locations and activities; life events in the past; time markers
12 page 67	Telephone language Things to do	Requests with *can* and *could*; object pronouns; *would*; verb + *to*	Telephone language; taking and leaving messages; chores

To the student

Welcome to *Talk Time*. Let's take a look at a unit.

Meeting people — Unit 1

name	nickname	first name	last name
address	e-mail address	telephone number/ phone number	apartment number

1 Speaking
Class CD Track 2

A Listen and look at the pictures. Then practice with a partner.

> A: What's your *name*?
> B: My name is Sun-hee Kim.

B What's your first name? What's your last name?
Tell your partner.

> My first name is Li-ting.
> My last name is Chen.

2 Listening
Class CD Track 3

People are asking questions. Listen and circle the correct answer.

1. **a.** 24 Green Street
   b. 617-555-0270

2. **a.** jbarnes@coolmail.com
   b. Jack Barnes

3. **a.** 312-555-7390
   b. 6A

4. **a.** 16F
   b. Willis

5. **a.** Blueman
   b. 735 Center Street

6. **a.** Chen
   b. bela@yakadoo.com

Unit 1   1

Each unit is divided into two lessons.
On the first page of each lesson you see:

Speaking

First you practice the new vocabulary for this lesson. You will listen to the CD, and look at the pictures. Then you practice using the new words with a classmate.

Listening

In this section, you listen to the vocabulary in short conversations and answer some questions.

On the second page of each lesson you see:

Grammar

In this section, you see the grammar focus for this lesson. You listen to the CD, and then practice the grammar.

---

3 Grammar: *Subject pronouns and possessive adjectives with be* Class CD Track 4

Listen. Then listen again and repeat.

I'm You're He's She's	a student.	We're They're	students.
It's	my nickname.		

What's **your** name?	**My** name is Matt.
What's **his** name?	**His** name is Ben.
What's **her** name?	**Her** name is Julia.

Memo
I am = I'm
you are = you're
he is = he's
she is = she's
it is = it's
we are = we're
they are = they're
what is = what's

4 Conversation Class CD Track 5

A *Pair work.* Listen to the conversation. Then practice with a partner.

A: Hello, I'm Jennifer. What's your name?
B: Hi, Jennifer. I'm Li-jun. Please call me Li. It's my nickname.
A: OK. It's nice to meet you, Li.
B: Nice to meet you, too. What's your last name, Jennifer?
A: It's Banks. What's your last name?
B: Wong.

B *Pair work.* Practice the conversation again. Give true answers about yourself.

Helpful Language
• How do you spell that?
• Please repeat that.
• Do you have a nickname?
• And what about you?

Extra
Talk to three more students. Write their first names, last names, and nicknames.

First name	Last name	Nickname
1. _____	_____	_____
2. _____	_____	_____
3. _____	_____	_____

5 Communication task: Address cards

A *Group work.* Talk to three classmates. Write your classmates' information on the address cards.

Address Card
First Name: _____   Last Name: _____
Nickname: _____   Phone: _____
E-mail: _____
Address: _____

Address Card
First Name: _____   Last Name: _____
Nickname: _____   Phone: _____
E-mail: _____
Address: _____

Address Card
First Name: _____   Last Name: _____
Nickname: _____   Phone: _____
E-mail: _____
Address: _____

B *Group work.* Compare the information on your cards. Ask and answer these questions.

Who has an interesting first name?
Who has a common last name?
Who has an interesting e-mail address?
Who has an interesting nickname?

Extra
Look at the address cards for one minute. Close your book.
What information can you remember? Tell your classmates.
A: *Mei's last name is...*
B: *Tamamo's phone number is...*

Conversation

In this section, you listen to a conversation and then practice with a partner. This lets you practice the vocabulary and grammar of the lesson in a larger context. It also lets you use your own information.

On the third page of each lesson you see:

Communication task

In this section, you practice the language of the lesson with a partner or a small group. This section lets you use your own information to speak more freely about the topic. Sometimes you and your partner will look at the same page, and sometimes you will look at different pages.

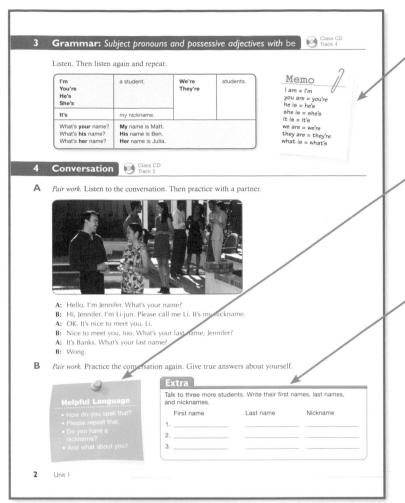

Other things you see in the unit:

Memo

The *Memo* reminds you about rules of English that are different from your language, for example, contractions. The language in the Memo will help you complete the activities.

Helpful Language

The Helpful Language note gives you questions or phrases that will help you complete the activities. They provide cues you can use to keep talking longer with your partner.

Extra

Sometimes you will see an Extra activity. This lets you practice more with the same language from the activity.

CD icon

The CD icon tells you that this activity is recorded on the audio CD, and your teacher may play it in class in order for you to do the activity.

Check your English

At the back of the book, there is a review page called *Check your English*. This page gives you a chance to review the language from the unit.

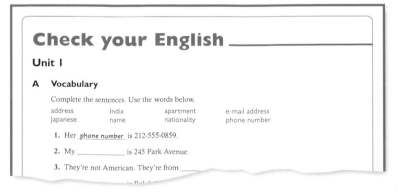

Every lesson gives you time to listen to English and time to talk with your classmates. *Talk Time* will help you increase your vocabulary and improve grammatical accuracy. I hope you enjoy studying with *Talk Time*. Good luck!

Meeting people

name

nickname

first name

last name

address

e-mail address

telephone number/
phone number

apartment number

1 Speaking
Class CD
Track 2

A Listen and look at the pictures. Then practice with a partner.

A: What's your <u>name</u>?
B: My name is Sun-hee Kim.

B What's your first name? What's your last name?
Tell your partner.

> My first name is Li-ting.
> My last name is Chen.

2 Listening
Class CD
Track 3

People are asking questions. Listen and circle the correct answer.

1. **a.** 24 Green Street
   b. 617-555-0270

2. **a.** jbarnes@coolmail.com
   b. Jack Barnes

3. **a.** 312-555-7390
   b. 6A

4. **a.** 16F
   b. Willis

5. **a.** Blueman
   b. 735 Center Street

6. **a.** Chen
   b. bela@yakadoo.com

Listen. Then listen again and repeat.

I'm You're He's She's	a student.	We're They're	students.
It's	my nickname.		
What's **your** name? What's **his** name? What's **her** name?	**My** name is Matt. **His** name is Ben. **Her** name is Julia.		

Memo

I am = I'm
you are = you're
he is = he's
she is = she's
it is = it's
we are = we're
they are = they're
what is = what's

---

4 **Conversation**
Class CD
Track 5

A *Pair work.* Listen to the conversation. Then practice with a partner.

A: Hello, I'm Jennifer. What's your name?

B: Hi, Jennifer. I'm Li-jun. Please call me Li. It's my nickname.

A: OK. It's nice to meet you, Li.

B: Nice to meet you, too. What's your last name, Jennifer?

A: It's Banks. What's your last name?

B: Wong.

B *Pair work.* Practice the conversation again. Give true answers about yourself.

Helpful Language
....
• How do you spell that?
• Please repeat that.
• Do you have a nickname?
• And what about you?

Extra

Talk to three more students. Write their first names, last names, and nicknames.

	First name	Last name	Nickname
1.	_____	_____	_____
2.	_____	_____	_____
3.	_____	_____	_____

A *Group work.* Talk to three classmates. Write your classmates' information on the address cards.

Address Card

First Name: [ ] Last Name: [ ]

Nickname: [ ] Phone: [ ]

E-mail: [ ]

Address: [ ]

Address Card

First Name: [ ] Last Name: [ ]

Nickname: [ ] Phone: [ ]

E-mail: [ ]

Address: [ ]

Address Card

First Name: [ ] Last Name: [ ]

Nickname: [ ] Phone: [ ]

E-mail: [ ]

Address: [ ]

B *Group work.* Compare the information on your cards. Ask and answer these questions.

Who has an interesting first name?
Who has a common last name?
Who has an interesting e-mail address?
Who has an interesting nickname?

Extra

Look at the address cards for one minute. Close your book.
What information can you remember? Tell your classmates.
A: *Mei's last name is...*
B: *Tamamo's phone number is...*

Countries and nationalities

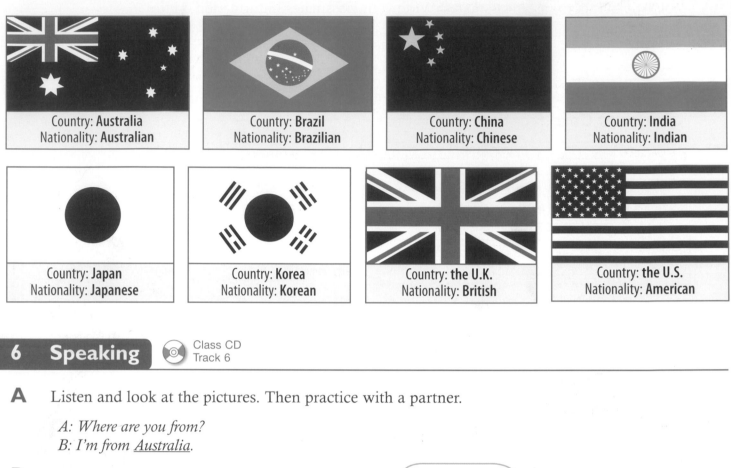

Country: **Australia**
Nationality: **Australian**

Country: **Brazil**
Nationality: **Brazilian**

Country: **China**
Nationality: **Chinese**

Country: **India**
Nationality: **Indian**

Country: **Japan**
Nationality: **Japanese**

Country: **Korea**
Nationality: **Korean**

Country: **the U.K.**
Nationality: **British**

Country: **the U.S.**
Nationality: **American**

6   Speaking   Class CD Track 6

A   Listen and look at the pictures. Then practice with a partner.

> A: *Where are you from?*
> B: *I'm from <u>Australia</u>.*

B   What nationality are you? Tell your partner.

> **I'm Korean.**

7   Listening   Class CD Track 7

> **Memo**
> who is = who's
> name is = name's

A   Who's meeting who? Listen and match the name tags.
Write the correct letter.

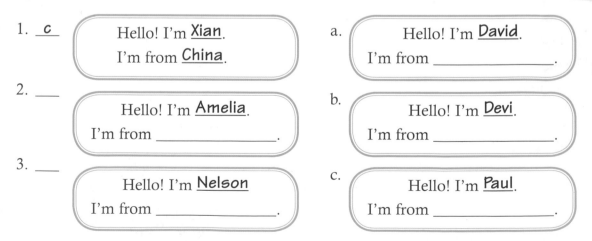

1. _c_

Hello! I'm <u>Xian</u>.
I'm from <u>China</u>.

a.

Hello! I'm <u>David</u>.
I'm from _____.

2. ___

Hello! I'm <u>Amelia</u>.
I'm from _____.

b.

Hello! I'm <u>Devi</u>.
I'm from _____.

3. ___

Hello! I'm <u>Nelson</u>.
I'm from _____.

c.

Hello! I'm <u>Paul</u>.
I'm from _____.

B   Listen again. Where are the people from? Write the countries on the name tags.

8 Grammar: *Yes/No questions and short answers with* be

Class CD
Track 8

A Listen. Then listen again and repeat.

Are you Korean?	**Yes, I am. / No, I'm not.**
Is he Indian?	**Yes, he is. / No, he isn't.**
Are you Brazilian?	**Yes, we are. / No, we aren't.**
Are they American?	**Yes, they are. / No, they aren't.**

Memo

is not = isn't
are not = aren't

B *Pair work.* Ask a partner questions about these people. Take turns.

Hongan Li

Maya Patel

Simon Baker

Mi-young Choi

Nicki Watts

Sumio Ito

Mateus Diaz

Jan and Mike Smith

9 Conversation

Class CD
Track 9

A *Pair work.* Listen to the conversation. Then practice with a partner.

A: Hi, are you in this class?
B: Yes, I am.
A: What's your name?
B: My name's Gina.
A: Nice to meet you. I'm Steve. Where are you from, Gina?
B: I'm from Brazil. How about you? Are you British?
A: No, I'm not. I'm Australian.

B *Pair work.* Practice the conversation again. Give true answers about yourself.

A Think of people who are in the news. Write their names below.

a business person

_____

a movie star

_____

an athlete

_____

a singer

_____

a politician

_____

an artist

_____

B *Pair work.* What can you say about each person? Score one point for each piece of information. Take turns.

> A: *He's a business person. He's American. His first name's Bill, and his last name's Cates.*
>
> B: *OK. Three points for you. Now it's my turn.*

Scorecard		
	My partner	Me
a business person		
a movie star		
an athlete		
a singer		
a politician		
an artist		
Total		

Family

1. husband
2. wife
3. father
4. mother
5. son
6. daughter
7. brother
8. sister
9. grandfather
10. grandmother
11. grandson
12. granddaughter
13. uncle
14. aunt
15. nephew
16. niece
17. cousin

1 Speaking
Class CD
Track 10

A Listen and look at the pictures. Then practice with a partner.

A: Who is Bill?
B: He's Nina's <u>husband</u>.

B *Pair work.* Talk about Nina's family.

Bill and Nina are Cindy's parents.

Memo
father + mother = parents
grandfather + grandmother
= grandparents
son + daughter = children
grandson + granddaughter
= grandchildren

2 Listening
Class CD
Track 11

People are talking about their families. Who are they talking about? Listen and circle the correct answer.

1. **a.** brother
   b. father

2. **a.** grandchildren
   b. children

3. **a.** parents and aunt
   b. grandparents and aunt

4. **a.** uncle and aunt
   b. grandparents and cousins

5. **a.** aunt and uncle
   b. niece and nephew

6. **a.** sister
   b. daughter

3 Grammar: Wh- *questions with be*

Class CD Track 12

Listen. Then listen again and repeat.

What's your name?	My name is Ken.
Where are you from?	I'm from New York.
How are you?	I'm fine.
Who's that?	That's my sister.
How old is she?	She's 16.
Who are they?	They're my parents.

Memo

who's he / she = who's that
that is = that's

4 Conversation

Class CD Track 13

A   *Pair work.* Listen to the conversation. Then practice with a partner.

Memo

If you have a husband or wife, you are married.

If you do not have a husband or wife, you are single.

A: Nice pictures. Hey, who's that?
B: That's my brother.
A: What's his name?
B: His name is Sung-ho.
A: How old is he?
B: He's 26.
A: Is he married?
B: No, he isn't. He's single.

B   *Pair work.* Draw a simple picture of someone in your family. Show the picture to a partner. Practice the conversation again. Give true answers.

Extra

Talk about your partner's picture again.
That's your sister. She's 19. Her name is

Communication task: My family tree

A   Draw your family tree.

Grandfather — Grandmother

Mother — Father   Uncle — Aunt   Uncle

Brother   Me   Sister   Cousin   Cousin

Helpful Language

• Who's that?
• What's his / her name?
• How old is he / she?
• Who are they?
• Is he / she married?

B   *Pair work*. Show a partner your family tree. Talk about your family. Your partner asks questions. Take turns.

Describing people

Height: tall
Weight: thin
Hair: short, curly, blond
Age: in his twenties
good-looking/handsome

Height: average height
Weight: average weight
Hair: short, straight, dark
Age: old

Height: average height
Weight: average weight
Hair: long, straight, dark
Age: middle-aged
pretty/beautiful

Height: short
Weight: heavy
Hair: long, straight, blond
Age: young
cute

6 Speaking
Class CD
Track 14

A Listen and look at the pictures. Then practice with a partner.

> A: Tell me about the boy. Is he _heavy_?
> B: Yes, he is.

> A: Is his hair _long_?
> B: Yes, it is.

B What are you like? Tell your partner.

I'm average height. I'm…

7 Listening
Class CD
Track 15

A Listen to the descriptions. Check (✓) the correct information for each person.

Hair		Height		Relationship	
1. ☐ blond	☑ dark	☐ average height	☐ tall	☐ mother	☐ brother
2. ☐ long	☐ short	☐ short	☐ tall	☐ son	☐ husband
3. ☐ blond	☐ dark	☐ average height	☐ tall	☐ cousin	☐ aunt
4. ☐ blond	☐ dark	☐ short	☐ tall	☐ sister	☐ daughter

B Listen again. Who are they talking about? Check (✓) the correct answer above.

8 Grammar: *Using* have

Class CD Track 16

A Listen. Then listen again and repeat.

Memo
do not = don't
does not = doesn't

I **have** straight hair.	I **don't have** curly hair.
She has blue eyes.	**She doesn't have** brown eyes.
Do you have short hair?	**Yes, I do. / No, I don't.**
Does she have long hair?	**Yes, she does. / No, she doesn't.**

B *Pair work.* Make sentences about yourself. Use *I have* or *I don't have.*

brown eyes	short hair	straight hair	dark hair
blue eyes	long hair	curly hair	blond hair

> **I have brown eyes. I don't have short hair.**

9 Conversation

Class CD Track 17

A *Pair work.* Listen to the conversation. Then practice with a partner.

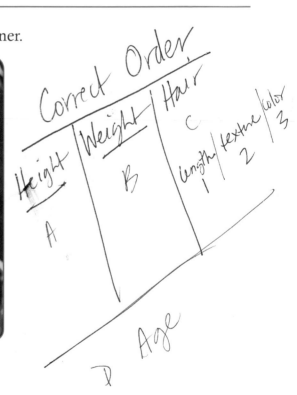

A: So, tell me about Dan. Is he good-looking?
B: Oh, yes. He's handsome.
A: Is he tall?
B: No, he isn't tall. He's average height.
A: Does he have blue eyes?
B: No, he doesn't. He has brown eyes and dark hair.
A: Does he have long hair?
B: No, he doesn't. His hair is short and curly.

B *Pair work.* Practice the conversation again. Give true answers.

Group work. Pretend you are a famous person. Don't say the person's name.
Partners ask Yes/No questions. The "famous person" gives short answers.

Yes, I am. / No, I'm not.
Yes, I do. / No, I don't.

A: *Are you Japanese?*
B: *No, I'm not.*
C: *Are you married?*
B: *Yes, I am.*
D: *Do you have dark hair?*
B: *Yes, I do.*

Extra

Describe a famous person. Don't say the person's name. Partners
guess who the person is.
A: *He's tall. He's thin. He's American. Who is it?*
B: *Is it…?*
A: *No, it isn't.*
C: *Is it…?*
A: *Yes, it is.*

In a classroom

1. a clock
2. a wall
3. a bulletin board
4. a board
5. an eraser
6. a ruler
7. an electronic dictionary
8. a pencil
9. a pen
10. a notebook
11. a desk
12. a chair
13. a floor
14. a wastebasket
15. a book
16. a table
17. a bookbag
18. a map

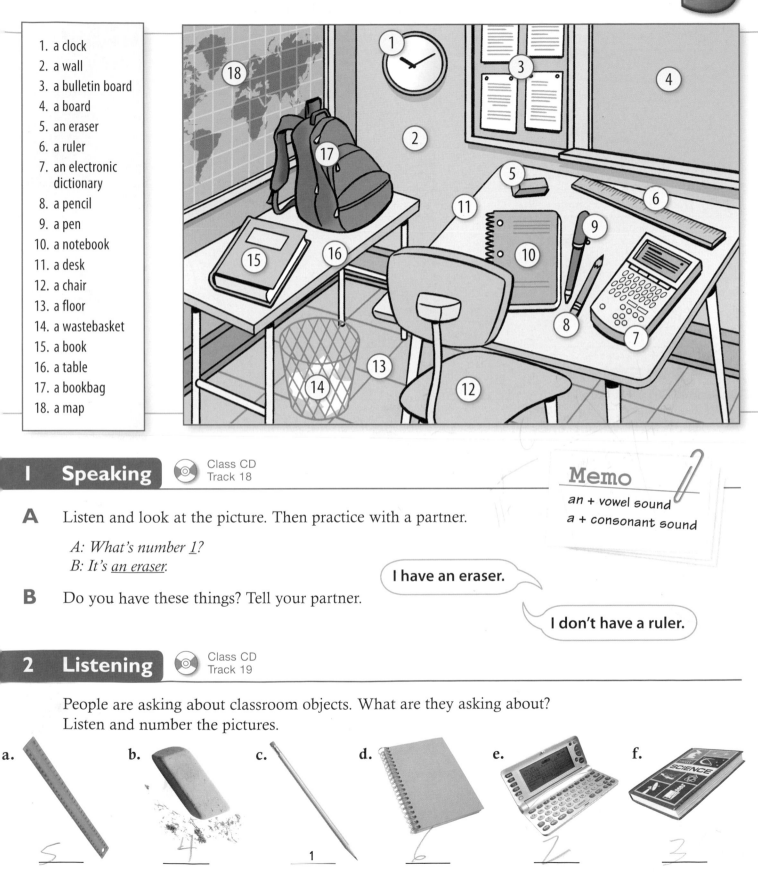

1 Speaking

Class CD
Track 18

A Listen and look at the picture. Then practice with a partner.

A: What's number 1?
B: It's an eraser.

B Do you have these things? Tell your partner.

I have an eraser.

I don't have a ruler.

Memo
an + vowel sound
a + consonant sound

2 Listening

Class CD
Track 19

People are asking about classroom objects. What are they asking about?
Listen and number the pictures.

a.
5

b.
4

c.
1

d.
6

e.
2

f.
3

3 Grammar: This / that; *preposition* on

Class CD
Track 20

Memo
Use *this* for an object near you.
Use *that* for an object far from you.

Listen. Then listen again and repeat.

This is a book. It's **on** the desk.

This is a notebook. It's **on** the table.

That's a clock. It's **on** the wall.

That's a wastebasket. It's **on** the floor.

4 Conversation

Class CD
Track 21

A *Group work.* Listen to the conversation. Then practice with two partners.

A: Is this your pen, Vicki?
B: No, it isn't. Ask Tim.
A: Tim?
C: Yeah?
A: Is this your pen?
C: Yes, it is. Thanks a lot!
A: No problem. And … is this your notebook?
C: Hmm. No, it's not. Where's your notebook, Vicki?
B: On my desk … Oh, no, it isn't. That's my notebook!

B *Group work.* Practice the conversation again. Use real names and real objects.

> **Extra**
>
> Take turns talking about objects in your classroom. Use *this*, *that*, and *on*.
> *A bulletin board is on the wall.*
> *That book is on a chair.*

Memo

spy = see

A   Listen and practice saying the letters of the alphabet.

Aa	Bb	Cc	Dd	Ee	Ff	Gg
Hh	Ii	Jj	Kk	Ll	Mm	Nn
Oo	Pp	Qq	Rr	Ss	Tt	Uu
Vv	Ww	Xx	Yy	Zz		

B   *Group work.* One person thinks of a thing in the classroom and says, "I spy something that begins with _____." Partners guess. The person who guesses right thinks of the next thing. It must be an object everyone can see.

A: *I spy something that begins with C.*
B: *Is it a clock?*
A: *No, it isn't.*
C: *Is it a chair?*
A: *Yes, it is.*

Extra

When you finish, look at a picture in this book.
Play "I Spy" using objects in the picture.

In an electronics store

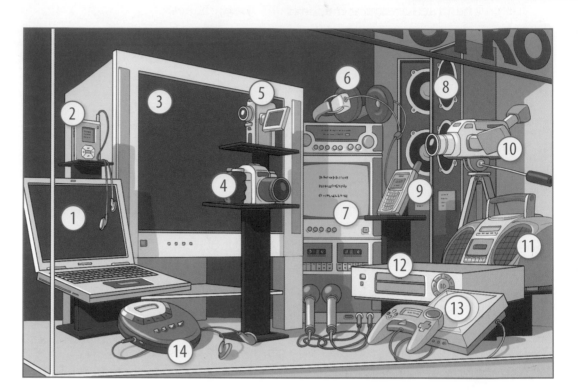

1. a laptop
2. an MP3 player
3. a television/ a TV
4. a camera
5. a digital camera
6. headphones
7. a karaoke machine
8. a speaker
9. a cell phone
10. a camcorder
11. a boom box
12. a DVD player
13. a video game system
14. a CD player

6 Speaking
Class CD Track 23

A Listen and look at the picture. Then practice with a partner.

A: *What's number 1?*
B: *It's a laptop.*

B Which items do you have? Which items don't you have? Tell your partner.

> I have a laptop. I don't have an MP3 player.

7 Listening
Class CD Track 24

A People are in an electronics store. What items are they talking about? Listen and number the pictures.

a.
Likes it ___
Doesn't like it ___

b.
Likes it ___
Doesn't like it ___

c.
Likes it ___
Doesn't like it ___

d.
Likes it ___
Doesn't like it ___

e.
Likes it ___
Doesn't like it ___

B Listen again. Do the people like the items? Check (✓) the correct answer above.

8 Grammar: These/those; *plurals*

Class CD Track 25

Memo
Use these for objects near you.
Use those for objects far from you.

A Listen. Then listen again and repeat.

These are clocks.

What **are these?**
They're cell phones.

Those are books.

What **are those?**
They're cameras.

B *Pair work.* Complete the conversations. Then practice with a partner.

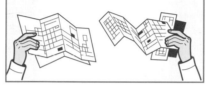

1. **A:** What _are those_ ?
   B: _They're camcorders_ .

3. **A:** What _are these_ ?
   B: _They're maps_ .

5. **A:** What _____?
   B: _____.

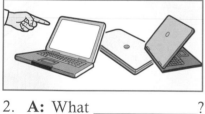

2. **A:** What _____?
   B: _____.

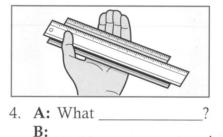

4. **A:** What _____?
   B: _____.

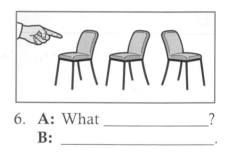

6. **A:** What _____?
   B: _____.

9 Conversation

Class CD Track 26

A *Pair work.* Listen to the conversation. Then practice with a partner.

A: May I help you?
B: Yes, please. Where are the CD players?
A: They're on the wall.
B: What are those?
A: They're DVD players. They're really good.
And these speakers are really good, too.
B: Are they expensive?
A: No, they're on sale.

B *Pair work.* Practice the conversation again.
Use different objects.

Student A looks at this page. Student B looks at page 73.

A   *Pair work.* Look at your picture. Then look at the items in the list. Where are these items in your partner's picture? Ask your partner. Then write the numbers of the items in the correct place in your picture.

1. a laptop
2. a cell phone
3. a wastebasket
4. maps
5. notebooks

A: *Where is the laptop?*
B: *It's on the…. Where are the headphones?*
A: *They're on the chair.*

B   *Pair work.* Show your picture to your partner. Are all the items in your list in the correct places?

> **Extra**
>
> Look at your picture for 30 seconds. Close your book. Tell your partner what you remember.
> *The laptop is…*
> *The headphones are…*

Everyday activities

sleeping	studying	reading e-mail	shopping
drinking	driving	cooking dinner	going to work
talking on the phone	playing the piano	washing dishes	taking a shower

1 Speaking
Class CD
Track 27

A Listen and look at the pictures. Then practice with a partner.

A: What's he doing?
B: He's sleeping.

> **What am I doing?**

> **You're playing the piano.**

B Act out an activity. Ask your partner, "What am I doing?"

2 Listening
Class CD
Track 28

Listen to the conversations. What are the people doing? Write the correct letter.

1. Mike _e_   **a.** shopping
2. Mary ___   **b.** studying
3. Jack ___   **c.** cooking dinner
4. Kim ___   **d.** reading
5. Susan ___   **e.** washing the dishes

3 Grammar: *Present continuous*

Class CD
Track 29

Listen. Then listen again and repeat.

I'm You're She's We're They're	eating.	I'm not You aren't She isn't We aren't They aren't	singing.
Are you Is she Are they	eating?	Yes, I am. Yes, she is. Yes, they are.	No, I'm not. No she isn't. / No, she's not. No, they aren't. / No, they're not.

Memo

You can also say:
You're not
He's not
We're not
They're not

4 Conversation

Class CD
Track 30

A *Pair work.* Listen to the conversation. Then practice with a partner.

A: Hello.

B: Hi, Sana. It's me, Nick.

A: Oh, hi, Nick.

B: What are you doing? Are you studying?

A: No, I'm not studying. I'm exercising. What are you doing?

B: Nothing much. Just reading my e-mail.

B *Pair work.* Practice the conversation again. Use your imagination. Pretend you are doing different activities.

Extra

Change partners. Practice the conversation with a new partner.

Student A looks at this page. Student B looks at page 74.

A Look at the picture. What can you see? Make notes.

A woman is playing the piano. A man is…

B *Pair work*. Your picture and Student B's picture are almost the same. Find out what is different. Ask what people are doing.

> **Extra**
>
> Look at Student B's picture on page 74 for 30 seconds. Then close your book. Can you remember what the people in the picture are doing?
> Say as much as you can about Student B's picture. Take turns.

Places

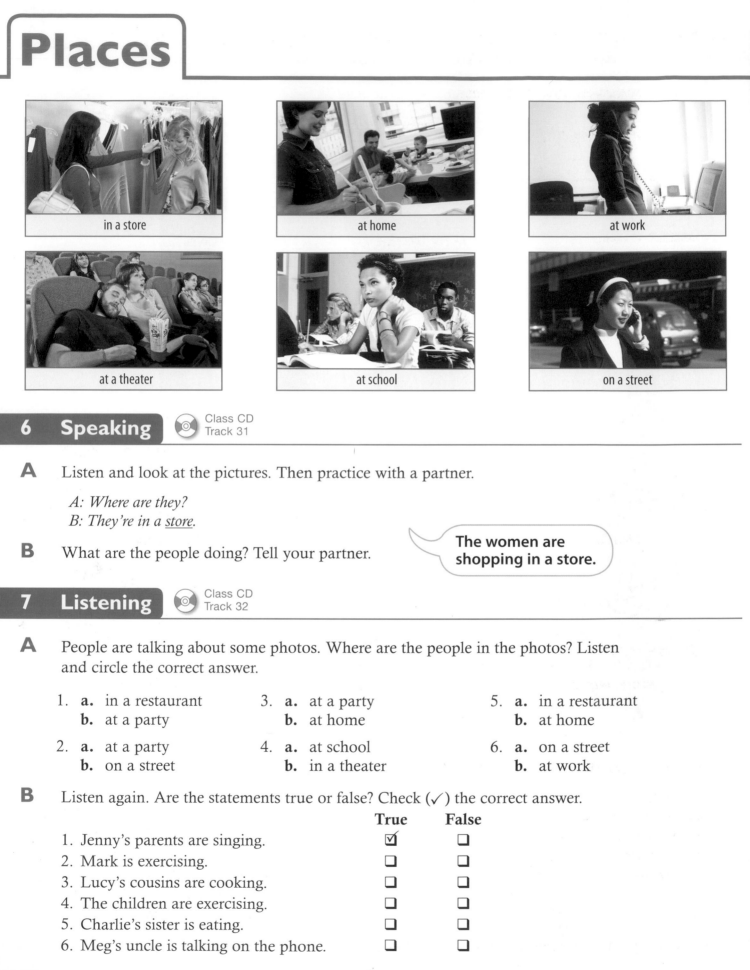

in a store

at home

at work

at a theater

at school

on a street

6 Speaking
Class CD
Track 31

A Listen and look at the pictures. Then practice with a partner.

A: Where are they?
B: They're in a store.

B What are the people doing? Tell your partner.

> The women are shopping in a store.

7 Listening
Class CD
Track 32

A People are talking about some photos. Where are the people in the photos? Listen and circle the correct answer.

1. **a.** in a restaurant
   b. at a party

2. **a.** at a party
   b. on a street

3. **a.** at a party
   b. at home

4. **a.** at school
   b. in a theater

5. **a.** in a restaurant
   b. at home

6. **a.** on a street
   b. at work

B Listen again. Are the statements true or false? Check (✓) the correct answer.

	True	False
1. Jenny's parents are singing.	✓	☐
2. Mark is exercising.	☐	☐
3. Lucy's cousins are cooking.	☐	☐
4. The children are exercising.	☐	☐
5. Charlie's sister is eating.	☐	☐
6. Meg's uncle is talking on the phone.	☐	☐

A Listen. Then listen again and repeat.

What's Eric **doing**?
Sleeping.
Where's he **sleeping**?
At home.

What's Beth **doing**?
Reading.
What's she **reading**?
Her e-mail.

Who's eating?
Paulo is.
What's he **eating**?
Dinner.

B *Pair work.* Ask a partner questions about the pictures. Use *who, what,* and *where* and the present continuous. Take turns.

Who's exercising? — John is. — What's Mai doing? — Talking on the phone.

John in Toronto

Mai in Ho Chi Minh City

Yusuke in Tokyo

Maria in Mexico City

Colin in London

Sunee in Bangkok

9 **Conversation** Class CD Track 34

A *Pair work.* Listen to the conversation. Then practice with a partner.

A: Hello.
B: Hi, Bart. It's Kate. What are you doing?
A: Studying. Where are you?
B: At home. So, tell me…what are you studying?
A: English. I have a big test.
B: Where's Ben? Is he at home?
A: Yeah, he is, but he's sleeping.

B *Pair work.* Practice the conversation again. Pretend you are doing different activities.

A *Pair work.* Describe the people in the picture and say what they are doing. Your partner asks Yes/No questions and tries to guess who you are talking about. Take turns.

> A: *This man is singing.*
> B: *Is he thin?*
> A: *Yes, he is.*
> B: *Is he short?*
> A: *Yes, he is.*
> B: *Is it Steve?*
> A: *Yes, it is.*

B *Pair work.* Ask your partner *Wh-* questions about the people in the picture. Take turns.

> A: *What's Cheng-han doing?*
> B: *He's singing. Who's talking on a cell phone?*
> A: *Suchada is. Where is…?*

Extra

Cover the picture. How much do you remember? Talk about the people in the picture. Say as much as you can about each person. Take turns.

A: *Cheng-han is singing. He's tall. He's…*
B: *Suchada is…*

Foods and drinks

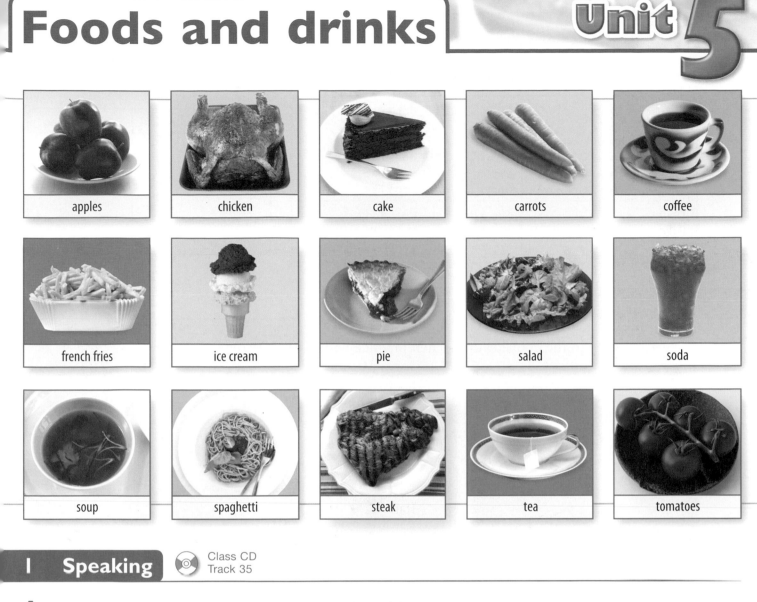

apples	chicken	cake	carrots	coffee
french fries	ice cream	pie	salad	soda
soup	spaghetti	steak	tea	tomatoes

1 Speaking
Class CD Track 35

A Listen and look at the pictures. Then practice with a partner.

A: Do you eat apples?
B: Yes, I do. / No, I don't.

B Which foods and drinks do you like?
Which ones don't you like? Tell your partner.

I like apples. I don't like carrots.

2 Listening
Class CD Track 36

A woman is in a restaurant. What does she order? Listen and check (✓) the correct answers.

Appetizers
❑ chicken soup
❑ tomato soup
❑ house salad

Main course
❑ roast chicken
❑ steak with french fries
❑ spaghetti with tomato sauce

Beverages
❑ tea
❑ coffee
❑ soda

Desserts
❑ apple pie
❑ carrot cake
❑ ice cream

3 Grammar: *Simple present; agreeing and disagreeing*

Listen. Then listen again and repeat.

I	like			I	don't like	
You	like			You	don't like	
He	likes	chicken.		He	doesn't like	steak.
She	likes			She	doesn't like	
We	like			We	don't like	
They	like			They	don't like	

Do you			Yes, I **do**.	No, I **don't**.
Does he	like	chicken?	Yes, he **does**.	No, he **doesn't**.
Do they			Yes, they **do**.	No, they **don't**.

	Agreeing		Disagreeing
I do,			I don't.
He does,	too.		He doesn't.
They do,			They don't.
I don't			
He doesn't	either.		
They don't			

4 Conversation

A *Pair work.* Listen to the conversation. Then practice with a partner.

A: Do you like Italian food?

B: Oh, yes. I love it!

A: I do, too. I know a nice Italian restaurant. It's called Luigi's.

B: Do they have pizza?

A: Oh, yeah. The pizza is great. And the spaghetti's good, too.

B: Where is it?

A: It's on Prince Street.

B: OK. Let's go!

> **Memo**
> let us = let's

B *Pair work.* Practice the conversation again. Talk about a restaurant you know.

Extra

What do you and your partner like to eat and drink?
Find two things you both like. Find two things you don't like.

A: *I like ice cream.*

B: *I do, too!*

A: *I don't like tomatoes.*

B: *I don't either.*

A   You are at the Sunshine Restaurant. Look at the menu. Circle the items you will order.

Sunshine Restaurant

Appetizers and Soups

Green salad   Chicken soup
Greek salad   Vegetable soup

Main Course

Fried chicken with french fries
Sirloin steak with mixed vegetables
Broiled fish filet with carrots
Spaghetti with meat sauce

Desserts

Apple pie   Mixed fruit
Chocolate mousse   Ice cream

Beverages

Coffee   Soda
Tea   Mineral water

B   *Pair work.* Take turns being a customer and a server. The server writes the customer's order on the order pad.

Sunshine Restaurant

Appetizer _____
_____

Main Course _____
_____

Dessert _____
_____

Beverage _____
_____

Helpful Language

Server:
• Are you ready to order?
• Can I get you an appetizer?
• And for your main course?
• Any dessert?
• Anything to drink?

Customer:
Can I have the _____?
I'd like the _____.

Snacks

chocolate	cookies	fruit	nuts
popcorn	potato chips	pretzels	rice cakes

6 Speaking
Class CD
Track 39

A Listen and look at the pictures. Then practice with a partner.

> A: Do you like <u>chocolate</u>?
> B: Yes, I do. / No, I don't.

> I like nuts and pretzels.

B What are your favorite snacks? Tell your partner.

7 Listening
Class CD
Track 40

A People are talking about snacks. What foods or beverages are they talking about? Listen and circle the correct answers.

1. **a.** soup   **b.** ice cream   **c.** tea
2. **a.** soda   **b.** popcorn   **c.** cake
3. **a.** cheese   **b.** chocolate   **c.** coffee
4. **a.** fruit   **b.** pie   **c.** salad
5. **a.** crackers   **b.** pretzels   **c.** nuts

B Listen again. What do you think each person says next? Circle the correct answer.

1. **a.** No, thanks.   **b.** She likes chocolate.
2. **a.** That's good.   **b.** No, thank you.
3. **a.** Yes, please.   **b.** Yes, I do.
4. **a.** Yes, he does.   **b.** No, I don't.
5. **a.** No, we don't.   **b.** No, we aren't.

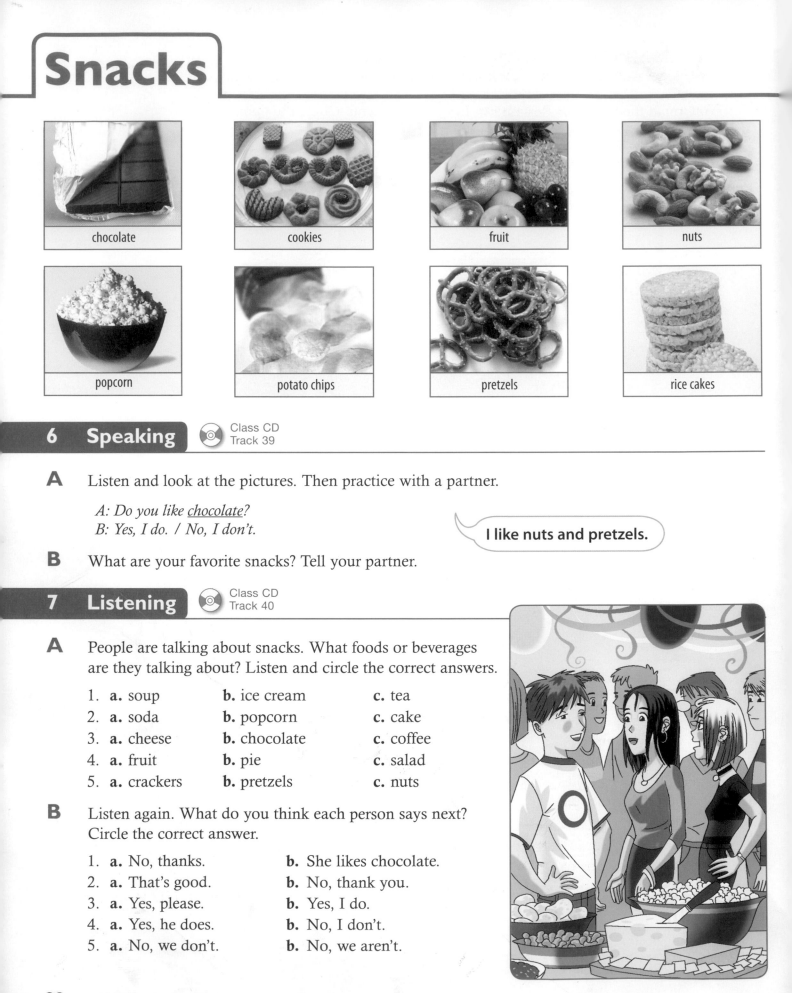

A   Listen. Then listen again and repeat.

Do you eat **much** popcorn?	No, not **much**.
I don't drink **much** coffee.	I drink **a lot of** tea.
How **many** pretzels do you eat?	**Not many**.
I don't eat **many** snacks.	I eat **a lot of** fruit.

B   *Pair work.* Ask a partner questions about these foods and drinks. Take turns.

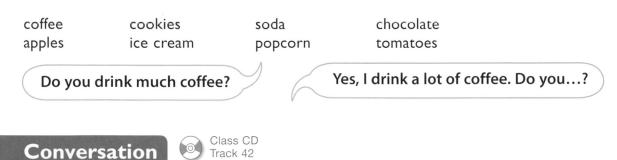

coffee   cookies   soda   chocolate

apples   ice cream   popcorn   tomatoes

Do you drink much coffee?

Yes, I drink a lot of coffee. Do you...?

9   **Conversation**   Class CD Track 42

A   *Pair work.* Listen to the conversation. Then practice with a partner.

A: Do you like chocolate?

B: I love chocolate! Do you like chocolate?

A: Yeah, I do. How much chocolate do you eat?

B: Oh, I eat a lot! I eat some every day.

A: Do you eat many chocolate bars?

B: No, I don't eat many chocolate bars, but I eat a lot of chocolate cookies and ice cream.

B   *Pair work.* Practice the conversation again. Give true answers about yourself.

> **Extra**
>
> Find three things your partner eats or drinks a lot.
> *Do you eat many...?*
> *Do you drink much...?*

A *Pair work.* Ask your partner questions about the people in the pictures. Take turns.

> A: *What is Hana eating?*
> B: *She's eating ice cream.*
> A: *How much ice cream is she eating?*
> B: *She's eating a lot of ice cream.*

Hana

John

Cara

Tan

Kayla

Jung

Taylor

Vicky

Ki-duk

B *Pair work.* Cover the pictures. Tell your partner about the people in the pictures. What are they doing? Say as much as you can. Take turns.

> A: *A woman is eating a lot of ice cream.*
> B: *A man is eating...*

Extra

Talk about your friends and family. What foods do they like? How much do they eat? What foods don't they like?
My father likes steak. He eats a lot of steak. He doesn't like...

Housing

1. living room
2. stairs
3. dining room
4. terrace
5. kitchen
6. garage
7. yard
8. balcony
9. bedroom
10. hall
11. closet
12. bathroom

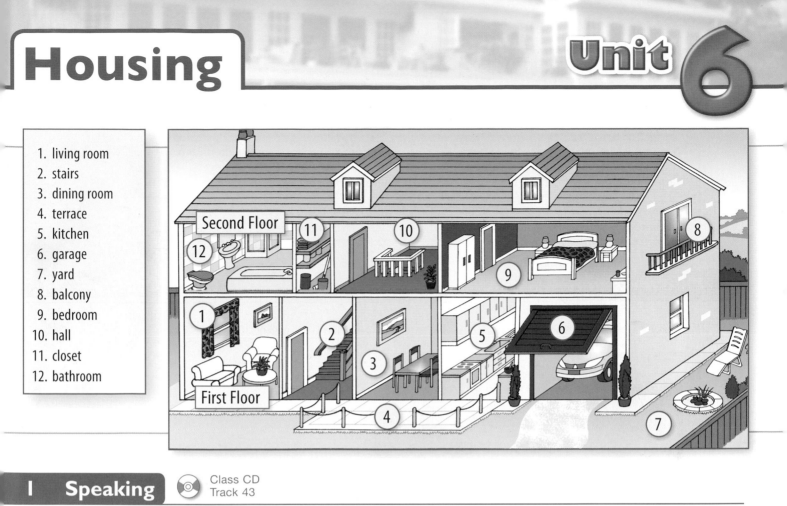

Second Floor

First Floor

1 Speaking
Class CD
Track 43

A Listen and look at the picture. Then practice with a partner.

A: *What's this?*
B: *This is the <u>kitchen</u>.*

B What's your favorite room? Tell your partner.

> **My favorite room is the living room.**

2 Listening
Class CD
Track 44

Which apartment are the people talking about? Listen and number the pictures.

a.

b.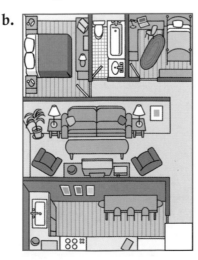

c.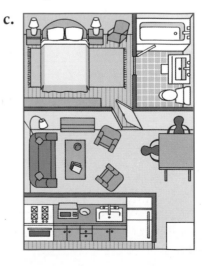

3 Grammar: There is / there are

Memo

there is = there's

Listen. Then listen again and repeat.

There's a bathroom on the second floor. **There's** no bathroom on the first floor. **There isn't** a bathroom on the first floor.	**There are** some closets in the bedroom. **There are** no closets in the hall. **There aren't** any closets in the hall.
Is there a yard? **Are there** any stairs?	Yes, **there is.** Yes, **there are.**	No, **there isn't.** No, **there aren't.**

4 Conversation

A *Pair work.* Listen to the conversation. Then practice with a partner.

A: Oh, I like your apartment, Daisy. It's really nice!

B: Thanks. I like it because it's big.

A: How many bedrooms are there?

B: There are two. And there's a living room, a kitchen, and a big bathroom.

A: Nice! And how many closets are there?

B: A lot. There are four big closets.

A: Wow! Is there a balcony?

B: No, there isn't, but there's a small yard.

A: That's great!

B *Pair work.* Practice the conversation again. Give true answers about your house or apartment.

Helpful Language

• Does it have a...?
• Where is the...?
• Where are the...?

Extra

Talk about your partner's home.
There are three rooms. There's a big bedroom. There's...

A Think about your dream house and answer these questions.

1. Where is it? _____

2. How many rooms does it have? _____

3. How many floors does it have? _____

4. What rooms are on each floor? _____

5. What special features does it have? _____

B *Pair work.* Talk about your dream house. Your partner asks questions. Take turns.

luxury apartment/in the city

house in the country

house on the beach

Helpful Language

• My dream house is on the beach.
• It has seven rooms.
• There are two floors.
• There's a big swimming pool in the yard.

Extra

Talk about your partner's dream house.
It's in the country. It has six rooms. There's a...

In an apartment

armchair

bed

picture

coffee table

dresser

lamp

bookcase

sofa

6 Speaking
Class CD
Track 47

A   Listen and look at the pictures. Then practice with a partner.

> *A: What's this?*
> *B: It's an <u>armchair</u>.*

B   What furniture is in your bedroom? Tell your partner.

> **There's a bed. There's a dresser.**

7 Listening
Class CD
Track 48

A   People are describing their bedrooms. What objects don't they have? Listen and number the items from 1 to 4.

___ bed   _1_ bookcase   ___ dresser   ___ lamp   ___ picture

B   Listen again. Are the sentences true or false? Check (✓) the correct answer.

	True	False
1. There is a picture on the wall.	❑	❑
2. There is a lamp on the floor.	❑	❑
3. She has a big bed.	❑	❑
4. He doesn't have much furniture.	❑	❑

Grammar: *Prepositions of place* 🔘 Class CD Track 49

A Listen. Then listen again and repeat.

The clock is **on top of** the TV.

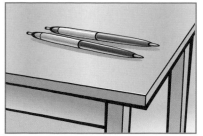

The pens are **on** the table.

The lamp is **between** the armchairs.

The wall is **behind** the sofa.

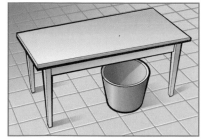

The wastebasket is **under** the table.

The lamp is **next to** the window.

B *Pair work.* Talk about objects in your classroom. Use prepositions of place.

> The dictionary is on top of the bookcase.

9 **Conversation** 🔘 Class CD Track 50

A *Pair work.* Listen to the conversation. Then practice with a partner.

A: What are you doing?
B: I'm looking for my cell phone.
A: It's on the bookcase, on top of the notebook.
B: Oh, right. And where are my books?
A: They're on the table.
B: The table under the window?
A: No, the table next to the sofa.
B: Oh, OK. I see them. Thanks!

B *Pair work.* Look at the picture. Practice the conversation again. Talk about where these things are.

clock   wastebasket   chair
plant   headphones

Student A looks at this page. Student B looks at page 75.

A   Look at the picture. Make notes about the things you see.

There's a table in the kitchen. There are three apples on the table.

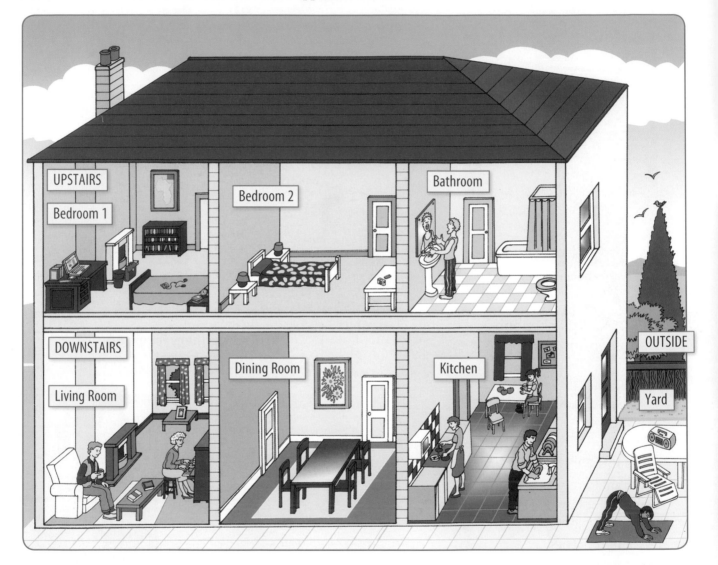

B   *Pair Work.* There are five differences between your pictures.
Tell your partner about the things and people in your picture.
Take turns. What are the differences?

1. _____

2. _____

3. _____

4. _____

5. _____

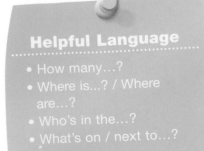

Helpful Language

• How many…?
• Where is…? / Where are…?
• Who's in the…?
• What's on / next to…?

Free time activities

go to the movies | watch TV | work out at a gym | surf the Internet

take photos | play cards | go dancing | go to the beach

go shopping | listen to music | eat out | paint

1 Speaking
Class CD
Track 51

A Listen and look at the pictures. Then practice with a partner.

A: What do you do in your free time?
B: I go to the movies.

B Which activities do you like to do? Which ones don't you like to do? Tell your partner.

> I like to go to the movies. I don't like to watch TV.

2 Listening
Class CD
Track 52

What do the people like to do? Listen and circle the correct answer.

1. **a.** eat out
   b. go to the movies

2. **a.** go dancing
   b. take photos

3. **a.** paint
   b. listen to music

4. **a.** work out at the gym
   b. go to the beach

5. **a.** surf the Internet
   b. watch TV

6. **a.** play cards
   b. go shopping

3 Grammar: *Information questions; adverbs of frequency*

Class CD
Track 53

Listen. Then listen again and repeat.

Do you **Does** Ken		work out?	Yes, I do. / No, I don't. Yes, he does. / No, he doesn't.
Where	**do** you **does** Ken	work out?	At a gym.
How often	**do** you **does** Ken	work out?	Three times a week/month. **Every day.** **Never.**
Who	**do** you	work out with?	With my brother.
When	**do** you **does** Ken	work out?	**On** Saturdays. **Every day.**

Memo

once = 1 time
twice = 2 times

4 Conversation

Class CD
Track 54

A *Group work.* Listen to the conversation. Then practice with two partners.

A: So, what do you do in your free time?

B: Well, I like to go shopping.

A: Really? Where do you go?

B: Anywhere. Big department stores, small stores … I just love to go shopping!

C: How often do you go?

B: Oh, about once a week.

C: Who do you go with?

B: Usually with my sister.

B *Group work.* Practice the conversation again. Give true answers about yourself.

Extra

Practice the conversation again. Use these phrases:

Really   *Anywhere*   *I just love to*
Oh, about   *Usually*

A   Think about three things you like to do in your free time.
Write your answers in the chart.

You

What do you do?	How often?	Who ... with?	Where...?
listen to music	every day	with friends	at home, at clubs

B   Ask your partner the questions. Write his or her answers in the chart. Take turns.

Your Partner

What do you do?	How often?	Who ... with?	Where...?
listen to music	every day	with friends	at home, at clubs

Extra

What do you and your partner both like to do in
your free time? Find two things you both like to
do. Find two things you don't like to do.

A: *Do you like to...?*   **A:** *Do you like to...?*
B: *Yes, I do.*   **B:** *No, I don't.*
A: *Me, too! / I don't.*   **A:** *Me neither. / I do!*

Helpful Language
- When do you...?
- Do you like...?
- Why do you...?

Popular sports

| volleyball | soccer | windsurfing | judo | cycling | snowboarding |

6 Speaking

Class CD
Track 55

A   Listen and look at the pictures. Then practice with a partner.

A: What sports do you like?
B: I like volleyball.

B   What sports do you like to play or do? What sports do you like to watch? Tell your partner.

> I like to play tennis.
> I like to watch soccer.

Memo

People **play**	People **go**
volleyball	skiing
basketball	ice-skating
soccer	windsurfing
tennis	swimming
baseball	cycling
golf	snowboarding

People **do**
judo

7 Listening

Class CD
Track 56

A   People are talking about sports. Match the people with the sports. Write the correct letter.

1. Wang ___   **a.** soccer
2. Molly ___   **b.** cycling
3. Jake ___   **c.** swimming
4. Sachi ___   **d.** judo
5. Dave ___   **e.** volleyball

B   Listen again. How often do the people play or do the sports? Check (✓) the correct answer.

	Every day	Once a week	Twice a week	Once a month	Never
1. Wang	❑	❑	❑	❑	❑
2. Molly	❑	❑	❑	❑	❑
3. Jake	❑	❑	❑	❑	❑
4. Sachi	❑	❑	❑	❑	❑
5. Dave	❑	❑	❑	❑	❑

Grammar: *Using* can *for ability* Class CD Track 57

A Listen. Then listen again and repeat.

I	**can**	play basketball.
She		cook.
I	**can't**	play tennis.
She		drive.
Can you	paint a picture?	**Yes, I can. / No, I can't.**
Can he	play baseball?	**Yes, he can. / No, he can't.**

B *Pair work.* Make sentences about yourself. Use *I can* or *I can't.*

dance   paint   play cards   do judo

play tennis   windsurf   cook   play basketball

Memo

can + not = can not
= cannot
= can't

> I can dance. I can't play tennis.

9 **Conversation** Class CD Track 58

A *Group work.* Listen to the conversation. Then practice with two partners.

A: What sports do you like?
B: I like basketball and tennis.
A: Yeah, me, too. Can you play tennis?
B: No, I can't …, but I like to watch it on TV. What about you?
    What sports do you like?
C: I like swimming and skiing.
B: Oh, can you ski?
C: Yes, I can. I go skiing every winter.

B *Group work.* Practice the conversation again. Give true answers about yourself.

A Answer these questions about yourself. Then add two questions of your own.

	You	Your partner
1. How often do you watch sports on TV?	_____	_____
2. What sports do you like to watch?	_____	_____
3. What sports don't you like to watch?	_____	_____
4. How often do you play or do sports?	_____	_____
5. What sports do you like to play or do?	_____	_____
6. What sports don't you like to play or do?	_____	_____
7. What sport can you play or do very well?	_____	_____
8. What's your favorite sport?	_____	_____
9. Who do you play sports with?	_____	_____
10. Where do you play sports?	_____	_____
11. _____	_____	_____
12. _____	_____	_____

B *Pair work.* Ask your partner the questions. Write the answers above. Take turns.

Life events

be born | start school | graduate | go to college

rent an apartment | get a job | date a boyfriend or girlfriend | fall in love

move | celebrate a birthday | take a vacation | travel

1 Speaking
Class CD
Track 59

A Listen and look at the pictures. Then practice with a partner.

A: What's he doing?
B: He's going to start school.

> I'm going to celebrate my birthday soon.

B Which events are going to happen to you soon? Tell your partner.

2 Listening
Class CD
Track 60

People are talking about important events. Listen and number the pictures.

a.

b.

c.

d.

Listen. Then listen again and repeat.

Are	you		**take** a vacation next month?	Yes, I **am**. I**'m going to take** a vacation in Thailand. No, I**'m not**.
Is	he	**going to**	**move**?	Yes, he **is**. He**'s going to move** to Hong Kong. No, he **isn't**.
Are	they		**rent** an apartment?	Yes, they **are**. They**'re going to rent** an apartment near the college. No, they **aren't**.

4 **Conversation** Class CD Track 62

A *Pair work.* Listen to the conversation. Then practice with a partner.

A: Are you going to take a vacation soon?
B: Yes, I am. I'm going to Hawaii.
A: Fabulous! Are you going to go with your parents?
B: No, my cousin is going to go with me.
A: How long are you going to stay?
B: Three weeks.
A: Wow! That's great.
B: Yeah, I'm really excited.

B *Pair work.* Practice the conversation again. Give true answers or use your imagination.

Extra

Close your book. Talk about a vacation you want to take.

A Look at the list of future time expressions. What are you going to do? Make notes.

I'm going to study English tomorrow.
I'm going to move in a few years.

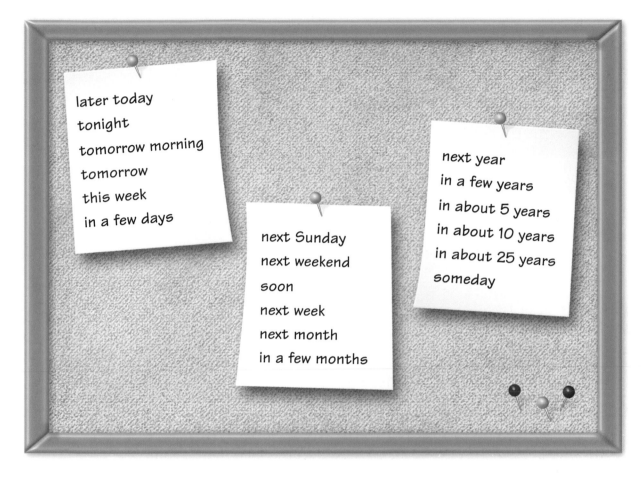

later today
tonight
tomorrow morning
tomorrow
this week
in a few days

next Sunday
next weekend
soon
next week
next month
in a few months

next year
in a few years
in about 5 years
in about 10 years
in about 25 years
someday

B *Group work.* Choose a future time expression. Use the expression to make a sentence about a future plan or event in your life. Partners ask questions. Take turns.

A: *I'm going to study English tomorrow.*
B: *Where are you going to study?*
A: *I'm going to study in the library.*
C: *Who are you going to study with?*
A: *With my sister.*

Weekend plans

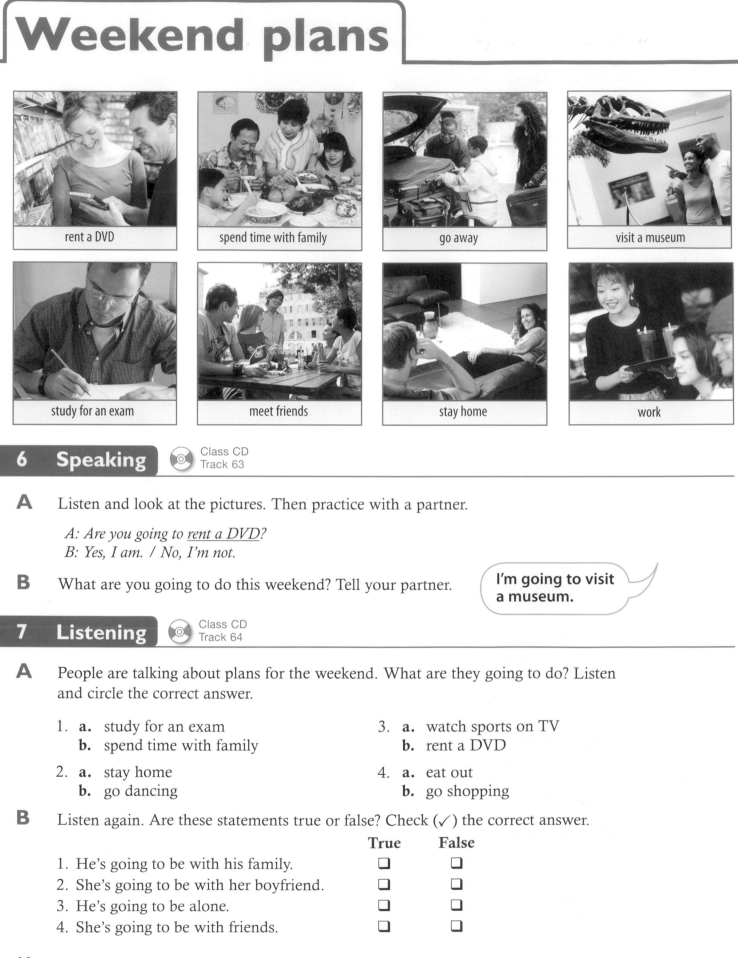

rent a DVD   spend time with family   go away   visit a museum

study for an exam   meet friends   stay home   work

6   Speaking
Class CD
Track 63

A   Listen and look at the pictures. Then practice with a partner.

> A: *Are you going to <u>rent a DVD</u>?*
> B: *Yes, I am. / No, I'm not.*

B   What are you going to do this weekend? Tell your partner.

> I'm going to visit a museum.

7   Listening
Class CD
Track 64

A   People are talking about plans for the weekend. What are they going to do? Listen and circle the correct answer.

1. **a.** study for an exam
   b. spend time with family

2. **a.** stay home
   b. go dancing

3. **a.** watch sports on TV
   b. rent a DVD

4. **a.** eat out
   b. go shopping

B   Listen again. Are these statements true or false? Check (✓) the correct answer.

	True	False
1. He's going to be with his family.	❑	❑
2. She's going to be with her boyfriend.	❑	❑
3. He's going to be alone.	❑	❑
4. She's going to be with friends.	❑	❑

8 Grammar: Wh- *questions with* be going to

Class CD
Track 65

A Listen. Then listen again and repeat.

What are you going to do on Saturday?		**visit** my parents.
Where are you going to be on Sunday?		**be** at home.
Who are you going to be with?	I'm **going to**	**be** with my brother.
When are you going to go away?		**go away** next weekend.
How long are you going to study?		**study** for two hours.

B *Pair work.* Ask and answer questions about the weekend. Use *what, where, who, when,* and *how long.*

9 Conversation

Class CD
Track 66

A *Pair work.* Listen to the conversation. Then practice with a partner.

A: What are you going to do this weekend?
B: I'm going to play tennis on Saturday.
A: Sounds like fun! Who are you going to play with?
B: With my friend Linda. We're going to play at the tennis club.
A: Great!
B: What about you? What are your plans for the weekend?
A: Nothing much. I'm going to stay home and read.
B: Sounds boring.
A: Not really. I'm reading a very interesting book.

B *Pair work.* Practice the conversation again. Give true answers about yourself.

> **Extra**
>
> Practice the conversation again. Try using these phrases:
> *Doing anything special?   Nothing much.   Fabulous!   Sounds like fun!*

A   Look at the activities below. Which of these things are you going to do this weekend?

B   *Class activity.* Ask your classmates what they are you going to do this weekend.
Find a classmate for each activity. Write the names and any extra information.

> A: *Are you going to go dancing this weekend?*
> B: *Yes, I am.*
> A: *Who are you going to go dancing with?*
> B: *My girlfriend.*

_____ is going to go dancing. (Find out who with.) _____	_____ is going to see a movie. (Find out what.) _____	_____ is going to eat out. (Find out where.) _____
_____ is going to meet a friend. (Find out who.) _____	_____ is going to watch TV. (Find out when.) _____	_____ is going to work. (Find out how long.) _____
_____ is going to go shopping. (Find out where.) _____	_____ is going to go to a party. (Find out where.) _____	_____ is going to play cards. (Find out with who.) _____
_____ is going to listen to music (Find out what kind.) _____	_____ is going to study (Find out how long.) _____	_____ is going to play a sport. (Find out what.) _____

C   *Group work.* Talk about what your classmates are going to do on the weekend.
Tell as many details as you can. Take turns.

*This Saturday night, Eun-young is going to rent a DVD. She's going to watch it
with her family at home.*

Movies

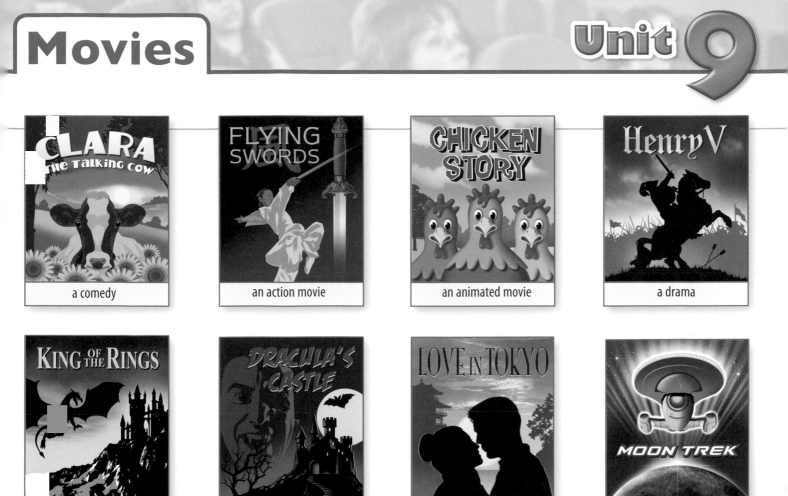

CLARA The Talking Cow — a comedy	**FLYING SWORDS** — an action movie
CHICKEN STORY — an animated movie	**Henry V** — a drama
King of the Rings — a fantasy	**DRACULA'S CASTLE** — a horror movie
LOVE in TOKYO — a romance	**MOON TREK** — a science fiction movie

1   Speaking
Class CD
Track 67

A   Listen and look at the pictures. Then practice with a partner.

A: Do you like comedies?
B: Yes, I do. / No, I don't.

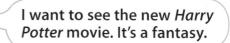

I want to see the new *Harry Potter* movie. It's a fantasy.

B   Name a movie you want to see. What kind of movie is it?
Tell your partner.

2   Listening
Class CD
Track 68

People are talking about movies. What kinds of movies do they talk about?
Listen and check (✓) the answers.

	Action	Comedy	Horror	Romance	Science fiction
1. Ben	❑	❑	❑	❑	❑
2. Liz	❑	❑	❑	❑	❑
3. Mike	❑	❑	❑	❑	❑
4. Sue	❑	❑	❑	❑	❑

Listen. Then listen again and repeat.

What kind of movies do you like?	I like **comedies**.
What kind of movies don't you like?	I don't like **horror movies**.
How often do you go to the movies?	I go **every week**.
When do you go to the movies?	I go **on weekends**.
What's your favorite movie?	My favorite movie is *Shrek*.
Why do you like comedies?	I like comedies **because** they're funny.
Who's your favorite actor?	My favorite actor is **Bruce Lee**.
Who's your favorite actress?	My favorite actress is **Audrey Hepburn**.

4 **Conversation** Class CD Track 70

A *Pair work.* Listen to the conversation. Then practice with a partner.

A: How often do you go to the movies?
B: Oh, once or twice a week.
A: When do you go?
B: I usually go on weekends.
A: What kind of movies do you like?
B: My favorite movies are action movies. How about you?
A: Well, I don't really like action movies. But I like horror movies a lot.
B: Really? That's surprising.

Memo

Saying what you like and dislike
☺ I love comedies.
☺ I like mysteries a lot.
☺ Action movies are OK.
☹ I don't really like science fiction movies.
☹ I can't stand horror movies.

B *Pair work.* Practice the conversation again. Give true answers about yourself.

Extra

Tell your partner about a movie star you really like. What's his or her name?
What kind of movies is he or she in? Why do you like him or her? Partners ask questions.
A: *I really like Bruce Lee. He's in a lot of action movies.*
B: *Why do you like him?*

A Think of your favorite movie. Look at the questions. Make notes in each box.

What's the name of the movie?
_____
_____

What kind of movie is it?
romance
and comedy

Who's in the movie?
_____
_____

What happens in the movie?
_____
_____

What do you like most about the movie?
_____
_____

B *Group work.* Take turns. Tell the group about your movie. Partners ask questions.

> My favorite movie is *Roman Holiday*. It's a comedy and a romance. Audrey Hepburn is in it. It's a story about a…

Helpful Language
- Is it an old movie?
- Is it an American movie?
- Where does the story take place?
- Why do you like it so much?

Extra

Talk about another movie you know. Don't say the name of the movie. Partners guess what movie it is.

A: *It's an animated movie. It's also a comedy.*
B: *Is it* The Lion King?
A: *No, it isn't.*
C: *Is it* Shrek?
A: *Yes, it is.*

TV programs

news

game show

cartoon

nature program

talk show

children's program

soap opera

sports

sitcom

reality show

---

6 Speaking
Class CD
Track 71

A Listen and look at the pictures. Then practice with a partner.

A: What TV programs do you like?
B: I like reality shows.

B What kinds of TV programs are you going to watch this weekend?
Tell your partner.

> I'm going to watch a sitcom and a
> game show this weekend.

---

7 Listening
Class CD
Track 72

A People are talking about TV programs. Listen and number the kind of programs
from 1 to 5.

___ cartoons   ___ game shows   ___ sitcoms   ___ news   ___ reality shows

B Listen again. Does the second speaker like to watch that kind of program?
Check (✓) *Yes* or *No*.

1. **a.** ❑ Yes   2. **a.** ❑ Yes   3. **a.** ❑ Yes   4. **a.** ❑ Yes   5. **a.** ❑ Yes
    b. ❑ No   **b.** ❑ No   **b.** ❑ No   **b.** ❑ No   **b.** ❑ No

A Listen. Then listen again and repeat.

Cindy **always** watches the news.
Akira **usually** watches cartoons.
Joy **often** watches nature programs.
Bob **sometimes** watches talk shows.
Ann **hardly ever** watches soap operas.
Ron **never** watches reality shows.

Do you **ever** watch sports on TV?	Yes, I **always** do.
	No, I **never** do.
Does Ya-ping **often** watch sitcoms?	Yes, she **often** does.
	No, she **hardly ever** does.
Does Jin-Won **usually** watch game shows?	**Sometimes** he does.
	He does **sometimes**.

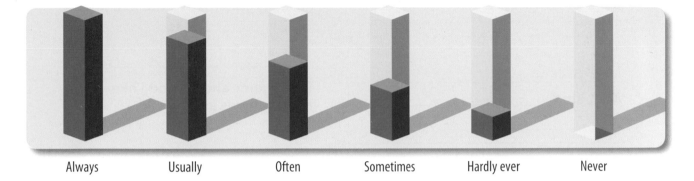

Always   Usually   Often   Sometimes   Hardly ever   Never

B *Pair work.* Ask and answer questions about these activities. Use *always, usually, often, sometimes, hardly ever,* and *never* in your answers.

watch cartoons on TV	listen to music at night	read in bed
eat out on Sunday	work out at a gym	go to the movies
get up at 6:00	speak English with friends	take a car to school

> **Do you ever watch cartoons on TV?**   **Yes, I often do.**

A *Pair work.* Listen to the conversation. Then practice with a partner.

A: Do you ever watch nature programs?
B: No, I never do. I really don't like nature programs.
    I usually watch talk shows and sports.
A: Oh, what sports do you usually watch?
B: Well, I watch baseball and basketball a lot. Do you ever
    watch sports?
A: Sometimes I do. But my favorite programs are sitcoms.
B: Hmm. Do you like cartoons?
A: Oh, yeah. I really like cartoons, too.

B *Pair work.* Practice the conversation again. Ask about different kinds of programs. Give true answers about yourself.

A   Look at the answers. Then complete the questions.

How often _____
_____?

I watch TV two or three times a week.

When _____
_____?

I usually watch TV in the evening.

What kind _____
_____?

I love game shows, and I like reality shows a lot.

What kind _____
_____?

I don't really like talk shows very much.

What _____
_____?

My favorite program is *Take a Chance*. It's a game show.

Why _____
_____?

The people and the questions are interesting.

B   *Pair work.* Compare your completed questions. Then ask your partner the questions. Make notes about his or her answers. Take turns.

C   *Group work.* Get together with another pair. Tell the group about your partner's answers. Take turns.

Keiko watches TV every day. She watches TV in the evening. She likes news programs and game shows. She doesn't like…

Health problems

| a headache | a stomachache | a toothache | a backache | an earache |

| a cold | a sore throat | a fever | a cough | the flu |

1 Speaking
Class CD
Track 75

A Listen and look at the pictures. Then practice with a partner.

  A: How are you today?
  B: I have a <u>headache</u>.

B Say what's wrong with the people in the pictures. Tell your partner.

> **She has a headache.**

2 Listening
Class CD
Track 76

People are talking about health problems. Listen and circle the correct answer.

1. **a.** a fever
   b. a headache

2. **a.** a cold
   b. a cough

3. **a.** a stomachache
   b. a toothache

4. **a.** an earache
   b. a backache

5. **a.** a sore throat
   b. a cough

6. **a.** the flu
   b. a cold

3 Grammar: Feel + *adjective*; have + *noun*

Class CD
Track 77

Listen. Then listen again and repeat.

Asking what's wrong		Saying what's wrong	
How	do you feel? are you?	I feel	sick. terrible.
		I don't	feel well.
What's	wrong? the matter?	I have	a headache. a cold. the flu.

Adjectives	
☺	☹
fine	sick
great	awful
terrific	terrible
better	worse

4 Conversation

Class CD
Track 78

A *Pair work.* Listen to the conversation. Then practice with a partner.

A: Hello?

B: Hi, Katy. It's Jeff.

A: Jeff? How are you?

B: Not so good. I'm afraid I can't meet you tonight.

A: Really? What's wrong?

B: I don't feel well. I have a sore throat.

A: Oh, I'm sorry to hear that. I hope you feel better soon.

B *Pair work.* Practice the conversation again. Use your imagination.

Helpful Language
....
• That's too bad.
• Oh, what a shame!
• Oh, no.

Extra

Try using these phrases with your partner.

go to the movies	*feel terrible*	*have a fever*
go dancing	*feel awful*	*have a headache*
go out to eat	*feel sick*	*have a stomachache*

Pair work. Number the sentences to make two conversations. Then practice the conversations. Take turns being A and B.

Conversation 1

Person A
____ Do you have a fever?
____ That's too bad. I hope you feel better tomorrow.
_1_ How are you today?
____ What's the matter?

Person B
____ I have a headache.
____ No, but I have a terrible backache.
____ Me, too.
_2_ Not so good. I feel terrible.

Conversation 2

Person A
____ Yes, and I have a stomachache.
_1_ How do you feel today?
____ I have a sore throat.
____ I don't feel so good.

Person B
_2_ I feel fine, thanks. How about you?
____ Maybe you have the flu.
____ Do you have a cough?
____ What's wrong?

Extra

Role-play a health problem.
Partners guess what the problem is.
Take turns.

a headache   an earache
a stomachache   a sore throat
a toothache   a backache
a fever   a cough
a cold   the flu

Getting better

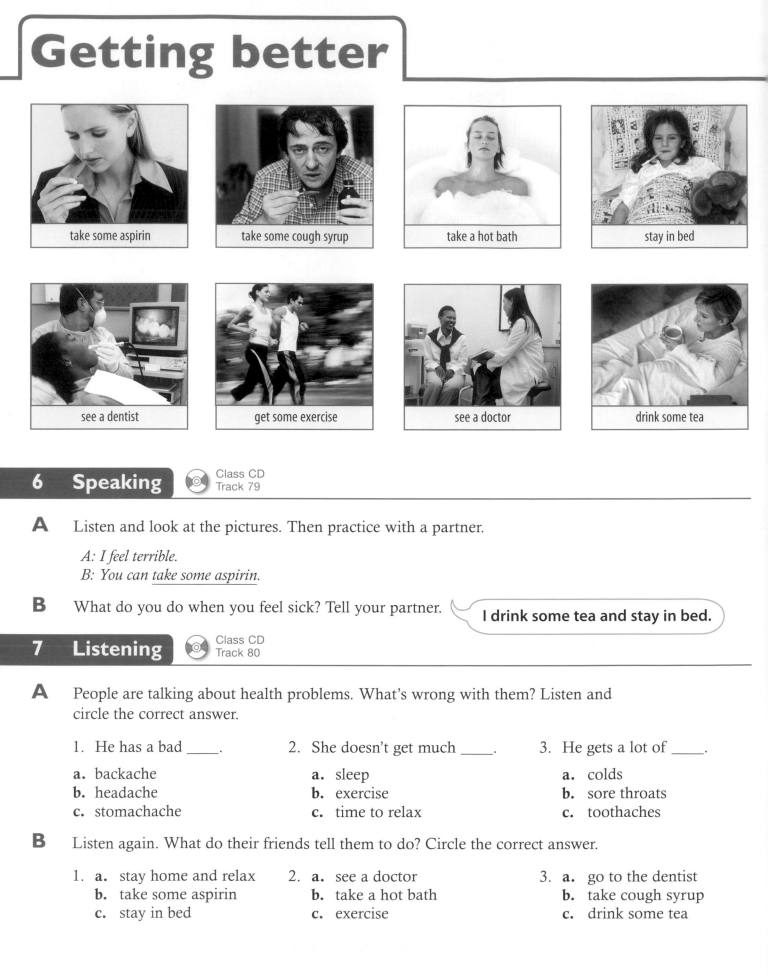

take some aspirin

take some cough syrup

take a hot bath

stay in bed

see a dentist

get some exercise

see a doctor

drink some tea

6 Speaking
Class CD
Track 79

A Listen and look at the pictures. Then practice with a partner.

A: I feel terrible.
B: You can take some aspirin.

B What do you do when you feel sick? Tell your partner.

I drink some tea and stay in bed.

7 Listening
Class CD
Track 80

A People are talking about health problems. What's wrong with them? Listen and circle the correct answer.

1. He has a bad ____.

  a. backache
  b. headache
  c. stomachache

2. She doesn't get much ____.

  a. sleep
  b. exercise
  c. time to relax

3. He gets a lot of ____.

  a. colds
  b. sore throats
  c. toothaches

B Listen again. What do their friends tell them to do? Circle the correct answer.

1. **a.** stay home and relax
  b. take some aspirin
  c. stay in bed

2. **a.** see a doctor
  b. take a hot bath
  c. exercise

3. **a.** go to the dentist
  b. take cough syrup
  c. drink some tea

8 Grammar: *Imperatives* 🔘 Class CD Track 81

A Listen. Then listen again and repeat.

Stay home and relax.	**Don't go** to school.
Drink lots of water.	**Don't eat** desserts.
Go to bed early.	**Don't work** too hard.

B *Pair work.* Complete the conversations. Use the sentences in the list or your own ideas. Then practice the conversations.

Don't work so hard.   Take some aspirin.   Drink a lot of juice.
Don't go to work.   See a dentist.   See a doctor.

1. **A:** I'm really tired.

    B: _____

2. **A:** I have a terrible toothache.

    B: _____

3. **A:** I get a lot of colds.

    B: _____

4. **A:** I think I have the flu.

    B: _____

9 Conversation 🔘 Class CD Track 82

A *Pair work.* Listen to the conversation. Then practice with a partner.

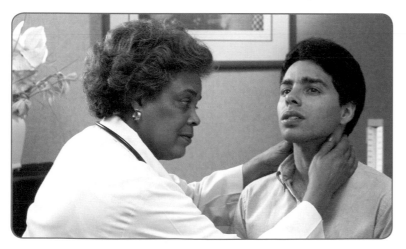

A: I don't feel so good, doctor.
B: What's wrong?
A: I have a sore throat and a cough.
B: Do you have a fever?
A: No, but I feel very tired.
B: It sounds like you have a bad cold. Take this cough syrup and get some rest. Drink lots of water. And don't work too hard.
A: OK, doctor.
B: And don't worry. You're going to be fine!

B *Pair work.* Practice the conversation again. Use your own information.

10A Communication task: Things you can do for a...

Student A looks at this page. Student B looks at page 76.

A *Pair work.* Think of two things you can do for each of the problems below. Write them in the chart.

Problem — Things you can do

1 You get a lot of colds.

2 You're always tired.

3 You have a sore throat.

4 You often get headaches.

5 You can't sleep at night.

6 You have the flu.

B *Group work.* Get together with another pair. Compare your ideas. What ideas do they have that you don't? Write the ideas in the chart.

On vacation

went to Guam	arrived on Tuesday	felt excited	rented a car
studied lots of maps	visited Tarzan Falls	went windsurfing	ate in restaurants
bought souvenirs	took photos	had a good time	came home

1 Speaking
Class CD
Track 83

A Listen and look at the pictures. Then practice with a partner.

A: Did they go to Guam?
B: Yes, they did.

B Talk about a vacation you took. What did you do? Tell your partner.

> I went to Australia.
> I visited...

2 Listening
Class CD
Track 84

People are talking about vacations. What did they do? Listen and check (✓) the answer. There is one extra.

	Stayed home	Went to Thailand	Went to the beach	Went skiing	Visited relatives
1.	❑	❑	❑	❑	❑
2.	❑	❑	❑	❑	❑
3.	❑	❑	❑	❑	❑
4.	❑	❑	❑	❑	❑

Listen. Then listen again and repeat.

Did you **go** to Vietnam?	No, I **didn't go** to Vietnam.
Where **did** you **go**?	I **went** to Hong Kong.
Who **did** you **go** with?	I **went** with my cousin.
What **did** you **do**?	I **went** to a karaoke club.
What **did** you **see**?	I **saw** the Tin Hau Temple.
What **did** you **visit**?	I **visited** the Museum of Art.
When **did** you **come** home?	We **came** home last Sunday.
Did you **enjoy** your vacation?	Yes, I **did**.
Did you **have** any problems?	No, I **didn't**.

Memo
did not = didn't

---

4   **Conversation**    Class CD Track 86

A   *Pair work.* Listen to the conversation. Then practice with a partner.

   A: Where did you go on vacation?
   B: I went to San Francisco with some friends.
   A: That sounds like fun. How long did you stay?
   B: Just one week. How about you? Did you go away?
   A: No, I didn't. I stayed home.
   B: Really? What did you do?
   A: Nothing much—I slept late. I visited friends. I went out to eat …
   B: Sounds like you had fun, too.

B   *Pair work.* Practice the conversation again. Use your imagination.

Extra

Write about three things you did on your last vacation and three things you didn't do. Use the verbs in the list or others. Then tell your partner about your vacation. Take turns.

Things I did on vacation	Things I didn't do on vacation
I went shopping.	*I didn't go swimming.*

go shopping	buy souvenirs	take photographs
go to the beach	stay home	visit a museum
visit relatives	go away	rent a car

A   Look at the questions below. Add two more questions. Make notes in the boxes.

1. When did you go on vacation? _in August_

2. Where did you go?
_____

3. How long did you stay?
_____

4. Who did you go with?
_____

5. What did you do?
_____

6. What did you see?
_____

7. What did you visit?
_____

8. What did you enjoy the most? _____

9. _____?
_____

10. _____?
_____

B   *Group work.* Tell the group about your vacation. Partners ask questions. Take turns.

> *A: My last vacation was in August. I went to Australia.*
> *B: How long…?*

Helpful Language
- Did you meet any people?
- What kind of food did you eat?
- What souvenirs did you buy?
- Did you take any good photos?
- How did you feel when you came home?

Past events

Hyun-ki was born in Pusan, Korea.

His family moved to Seoul when he was three.

He grew up in Seoul.

He started school when he was five.

He attended high school in Seoul.

He graduated from high school two years ago.

He took a trip to Australia in 2006.

He entered college when he was 18.

6 Speaking
Class CD
Track 87

A Listen and look at the pictures. Then practice with a partner.

A: Where was he born?
B: He was born in Pusan.

B Think about three or more events in your past. Use some of the verbs above. Tell your partner.

I was born in Taipei. I grew up in…

7 Listening
Class CD
Track 88

A People are talking about past events in their lives. Listen and number the pictures.

a.

b.

c.

d.

a. last week
b. yesterday

a. two years ago
b. three years ago

a. when she was five
b. when she was four

a. last week
b. last month

B Listen again. When did the events happen? Circle the correct answer above.

A Listen. Then listen again and repeat.

When **were you** born?	**I was** born in 1987.
Were you born in the U.S.?	No, **I wasn't**.
Where **were you** born?	**I was** born in Japan.
Was your sister born in Japan?	Yes, **she was**.
What city **was she** born in?	**She was** born in Osaka.
Were your parents born in Osaka?	No, **they weren't**.
Where **were they** born?	**They were** born in Nagoya.
Were your grandparents from Nagoya?	Yes, **they were**.
Was your grandfather Japanese?	Yes, **he was**.

Memo
was not = wasn't
were not = weren't

B *Pair work.* Ask your partner questions about past events in his or her life. Take turns.

A *Pair work.* Listen to the conversation. Then practice with a partner.

A: Do you remember your first boyfriend, Emi?
B: Oh, sure. I remember him. He was really cute!
A: Where was he from?
B: He was from Australia. We were so in love!
A: No kidding? How old were you?
B: I was 15. And he was about 16.
A: What was his name?
B: You know what? I can't remember!

B *Pair work.* Practice the conversation again. This time ask about a best friend in school. Give true answers about yourself.

Do you remember your best friend in school?

Extra

Tell your partner about a person you remember from your childhood: a teacher, a relative, a friend, or another person who was important to you.

Who was the person? What was his / her name? How old were you when you met him / her? What was he / she like? Why do you remember the person?

A Think about a happy event in your life. It can be something that happened a long time ago or very recently. Make notes about the event in the chart.

	Your event	Your partner's event
What was the event?		
Where were you?		
How old were you?		
Who was with you?		
Why were you so happy?		
What else can you say about the event?		

B *Pair work.* Tell your partner about your happy event. Your partner takes notes and asks questions to get more information. Take turns.

C *Class activity.* Tell the class about your partner's happy event.

Helpful Language
- Did you...?
- How long did you...?
- Why did you...?
- How did you feel?

Telephone language | Unit 12

Leaving messages

answering machine

Hello, this is Yu-mi. I'm sorry, but I can't come to the phone right now. Please leave a message after the beep.

Hi, Yu-mi. This is Mark. I have a question about the homework. Can you call me? My number is 918-555-7023. Bye.

leave a message

text message

Yu-Mi, Please call me, 918-555-7023, Mark

Taking messages

Hi. Is Dave there?

Who's calling, please?

make a phone call

This is Miki Ono.

introduce yourself

Dave's not here. But he's going to be home any minute now.

Do you want to leave a message?

Dave, Miki Ono called

take a message

Yes. Please tell him I called.

1 Speaking
Class CD Track 91

A Listen and look at the pictures. Then practice with a partner.

A: Do you have an <u>answering machine</u>?
B: Yes, I do. / No, I don't.

B Call your partner and leave a message.

Who's calling, please?

This is Miki Ono.

2 Listening
Class CD Track 92

Why can't the people come to the phone? Listen and circle the correct answer.

1. **a.** He's in the shower.
   b. He's at work.

2. **a.** She's at school.
   b. She's on a trip.

3. **a.** He's sleeping.
   b. He's at the library.

4. **a.** She's very sick.
   b. She's not at home.

Listen. Then listen again and repeat.

Can and *could* in requests	
Can I speak to Justin?	He's in the shower. **Can** you call back later?
Could I please speak to Emma?	She's in class. **Can** I take a message?
Object pronouns	
Please give **me** the number. I don't have **it**.	
Please give **her** a message. Ask **her** to call me.	
You can call **him** at work. I'll give **him** the message.	
Please ask **them** to call **us**.	

Subject pronouns	Object pronouns
I	me
you	you
he	him
she	her
it	it
we	us
they	them

4 **Conversation** Class CD
Track 94

A *Pair work.* Listen to the conversation. Then practice with a partner.

A: Hello.

B: Hi, Julie. It's Ted. Can I please speak to Michelle?

A: Oh, hi, Ted. Michelle isn't here right now. She's at the library.

B: Well, could you please take a message?

A: Sure. What's the message?

B: Ask her to call me at my brother's house.

A: OK. Just give me the number.

B: It's 314-555-0859.

A: 314-555-0859. Right?

B: Yes, that's it. Thanks a lot, Julie.

A: OK. Bye.

B *Pair work.* Practice the conversation again. Use different names and information.

Extra

Change partners. Practice the conversation
again with your new partner.

A   *Pair work.* Number the sentences to make a phone conversation. Then practice the conversation. Take turns being A and B.

Person A

___ You're welcome. Good-bye.

_1_ Hello.

___ OK. I'll give him the message.

___ Sure. What's the phone number?

___ Oh, hi, Sally. I'm sorry, Greg's not at home right now. Can I take a message?

Person B

___ It's 212-555-0859.

___ Thank you.

___ Good-bye

___ Yes, please. Could you ask him to call me at work?

_2_ Hi, Jeff. This is Sally. Can I speak to Greg, please?

B   *Pair work.* Role-play having a conversation on the phone. Follow the directions below. Take turns being A and B.

A

1. Answer the phone.
3. Tell **B** you're sorry. Judy isn't at home right now. Ask if you can take a message.
5. Say, "OK." Ask if Judy has **B's** number at work.
7. Say, "OK." Tell **B** you'll give Judy the message.
9. Say, "You're welcome" and "Good-bye."

B

2. Greet **A** and ask to speak to Judy.
4. Say, "Yes." Ask **A** to tell Judy to call you at work.
6. Say, "Yes, she does."
8. Thank **A**.
10. Say, "Good-bye."

Things to do

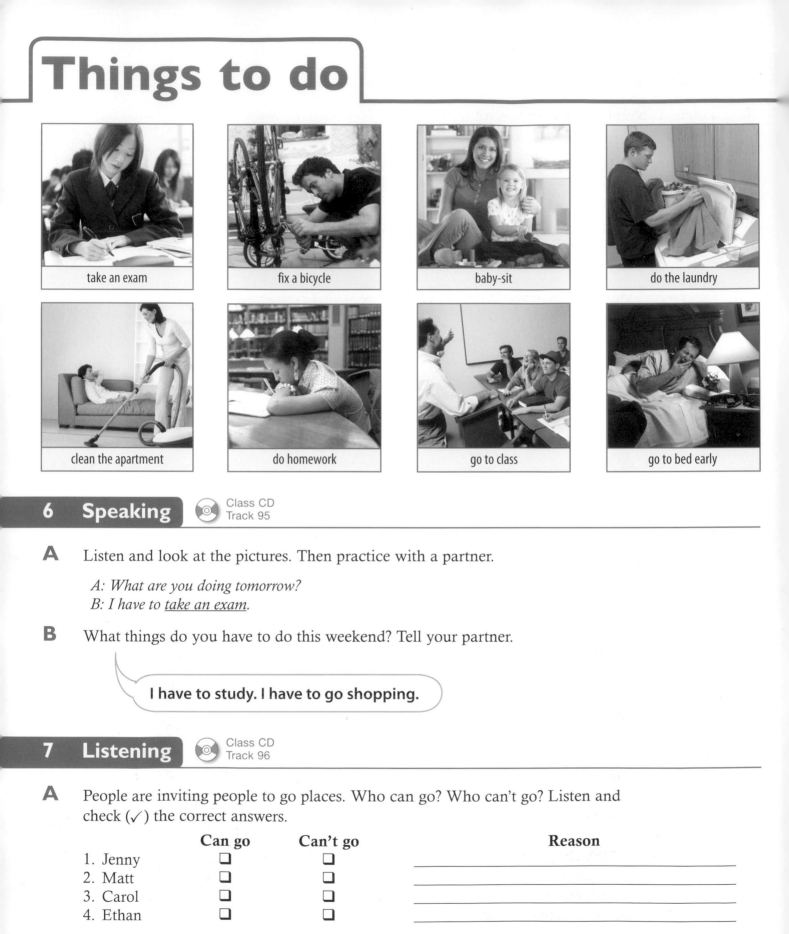

take an exam	fix a bicycle	baby-sit	do the laundry
clean the apartment	do homework	go to class	go to bed early

6 Speaking

Class CD
Track 95

A Listen and look at the pictures. Then practice with a partner.

A: What are you doing tomorrow?
B: I have to <u>take an exam</u>.

B What things do you have to do this weekend? Tell your partner.

> I have to study. I have to go shopping.

7 Listening

Class CD
Track 96

A People are inviting people to go places. Who can go? Who can't go? Listen and check (✓) the correct answers.

	Can go	Can't go	Reason
1. Jenny	☐	☐	_____
2. Matt	☐	☐	_____
3. Carol	☐	☐	_____
4. Ethan	☐	☐	_____

B Listen again. For the people who can't go, what reason do they give? Write it on the correct line above.

Class CD
Track 97

A Listen. Then listen again and repeat.

Would you **like to** see a movie tomorrow night?	Yes, **I'd love to**.
Would you **like to** go out to dinner with me tonight?	**I'd like to**, but I can't. I **have to** work late.
Do you **want to** go to a concert on Friday night?	I can't. I **need to baby-sit** my little sister.
Do you **want to** go to the soccer game on Saturday?	Sorry. I really **want to**, but I can't. I **have to** go to the dentist.

Memo
I would = I'd
I have to = I must
I've got to = I must

B *Pair work.* Complete the conversations. Then practice with a partner. In some places, more than one answer is possible.

1. **A:** ____Would____ you like ____to____ go swimming on Saturday?

   B: I'm sorry, I ____can't____. I ____have to____ go to the dentist.

2. **A:** _____ you want _____ go shopping tomorrow?

   B: I'd _____, but I can't. I _____ work late.

3. **A:** Would you _____ to see a play on Sunday?

   B: I can't. I _____ baby-sit.

4. **A:** Do you _____ to go to a party on Friday night?

   B: Yes, I'd _____!

Class CD
Track 98

A *Pair work.* Listen to the conversation. Then practice with a partner.

A: Hello?

B: Hello, Laura? This is In-sook.

A: In-sook! How are you?

B: I'm fine. How are you?

A: Great!

B: Listen. Would you like to come over for dinner on Friday? I'm making Korean food.

A: I'd love to. What time do you want me to come?

B: Oh, about 7:00. Do you have my address?

A: No, I don't. What is it?

B: It's 238 Park Street.

A: 238 Park Street. OK. See you on Friday!

B *Pair work.* Practice the conversation again. Use different names and information.

Class activity. Invite people to do the things in the pictures or use your own ideas.
Write your activities in the calendar. For every day, meet with a different classmate.

A: *Akira, would you like to see a movie on Monday?*
B: *I'd love to. Thanks.*
A: *Emy, do you want to go to the gym with me on Tuesday?*
C: *I'm sorry, I can't. I've got to do homework.*

21 Monday	22 Tuesday	23 Wednesday		24 Thursday	25 Friday	26 Saturday
						27 Sunday

Extra

Pair work. Tell a partner about your plans for the week.
On Monday, I'm going to see a movie with Akira. On Tuesday, I'm...

Student B looks at this page. Student A looks at page 18.

A   *Pair work.* Look at your picture. Then look at the items in the list. Where are these items in your partner's picture? Ask your partner. Then write the numbers of the items in the correct place in your picture.

1. headphones   4. books
2. clock   5. camera
3. television

> *A: Where is the laptop?*
> *B: It's on the table. Where are the headphones?*
> *A: They're…*

B   *Pair work.* Show your picture to your partner. Are all the items in your list in the correct places?

Extra

Look at your picture for 30 seconds. Close your book. Tell your partner what you remember.
The laptop is…
The headphones are…

Student B looks at this page. Student B looks at page 21.

A   Look at the picture. What can you see? Make notes.

A man is playing the piano. A woman is…

B   *Pair work.* Your picture and Student A's picture are almost the same. Find out what is different. Ask what people are doing.

Extra

Look at Student A's picture on page 21 for 30 seconds. Then close your book. Can you remember what the people in the picture are doing?
Say as much as you can about Student B's picture. Take turns.

Student B looks at this page. Student A looks at page 36.

A Look at the picture. Make notes about the things you see.

There's a table in the kitchen. There are three apples on the table.

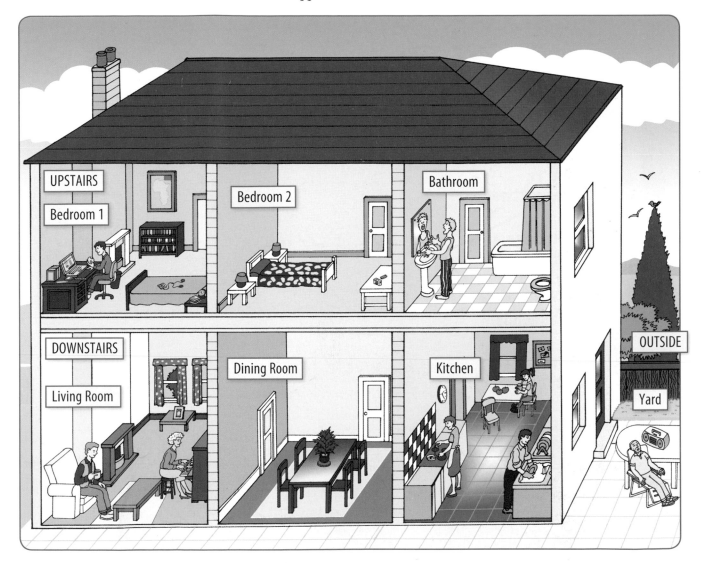

B *Pair Work.* There are five differences between your pictures. Tell your partner about the things and people in your picture. Take turns. What are the differences?

1. _____

2. _____

3. _____

4. _____

5. _____

Helpful Language
....
- How many…?
- Where is…? / Where are…?
- Who's in the…?
- What's on / next to…?

Student A looks at this page. Student B looks at page 60.

A *Pair work.* Think of two things you can do for each of the problems below. Write them in the chart.

Problem   Things you can do

1 You get a lot
of colds.   _____   _____

                          _____   _____

2 You're
always tired.   _____   _____

                          _____   _____

3 You have a
sore throat.   _____   _____

                          _____   _____

4 You often get
headaches.   _____   _____

                          _____   _____

5 You can't
sleep at night.   _____   _____

                          _____   _____

6 You have
the flu.   _____   _____

                          _____   _____

B *Group work.* Get together with another pair. Compare your ideas. What ideas do they have that you don't? Write the ideas in the chart.

Check your English

Unit 1

A Vocabulary

Complete the sentences. Use the words below.

address   India   apartment   e-mail address
Japanese   name   nationality   phone number

1. Her _phone number_ is 212-555-0859.

2. My _____ is 245 Park Avenue.

3. They're not American. They're from _____.

4. His _____ is Ralph Lee.

5. What is your _____ number? It's 54.

6. Happymoon@horizon.com is my _____.

7. She's _____.

8. What _____ are you?

B Grammar

Match the questions with the answers.

1. Nice to meet you. _d_

2. What's his name? ___

3. Where are Silvia and Paulo from? ___

4. Is Rodney American? ___

5. Are Uma and Sanjay from India? ___

6. Hi, I'm Nelson. ___

7. Are you from Korea? ___

a. James Bond.

b. Brazil.

c. Yes, they are.

d. It's nice to meet you, too.

e. No, he isn't. He's British.

f. Yes, I am.

g. Nice to meet you, Nelson.

Check your English _____

Unit 2

A Vocabulary

Read the sentences. Complete the words.

1. She's nine years old. She's <u>y</u> <u>o</u> <u>u</u> <u>n</u> <u>g</u>.

2. They have two children—a daughter and a <u>s</u> _ _.

3. He's very good-looking. He's <u>h</u> _ <u>n</u> _ _ <u>s</u> _ <u>m</u> _.

4. Your mother's brother is your <u>u</u> _ <u>c</u> _ _.

5. Her hair isn't long. It's _ <u>h</u> _ _ <u>t</u>.

6. My father is 53. He's <u>m</u> _ <u>d</u> _ <u>l</u> _ - <u>a</u> _ _ <u>d</u>.

7. She's married. Sam is her _ <u>u</u> _ <u>b</u> _ <u>n</u> _.

8. I'm not short. I'm not tall. I'm _ <u>v</u> _ <u>r</u> _ <u>g</u> _ <u>h</u> _ _ <u>g</u> <u>h</u> _.

B Grammar

Complete the questions.

1. **A:** <u>Where</u> is she from?
   B: She's from Australia.

2. **A:** _____ is he?
   B: He's 21.

3. **A:** _____ are they?
   B: They're my cousins.

4. **A:** _____ he have dark hair?
   B: No, he has blond hair.

5. **A:** _____ are you?
   B: I'm fine.

6. **A:** _____ that?
   B: That's my grandmother.

7. **A:** _____ you have a sister?
   B: Yes, I do.

8. **A:** _____ she married?
   B: No, she isn't.

Check your English

Unit 3

A Vocabulary

Read the definitions. Write the correct words.

camcorder   eraser   cell phone   desk
headphones   map   DVD player   karaoke machine

1. Something you use to talk to someone who is in a different place   <u>cell phone</u>

2. A drawing of a town, a country, or the world ___map___

3. Things you wear over your ears to listen to something ___headphones___

4. Thing you use to take away marks on paper or a board ___eraser___

5. A machine you can use to watch movies ___DVD player___

6. Something you use to videotape pictures and sound ___Camcorder___

7. A machine you use to play music that you sing along to ___Karaoke machine___

8. A table that you sit at to write or work ___desk___

B Grammar

Finish the questions. Write the correct word. Then match the questions with the answers.

are   is   this   those   what   where

1. <u>What</u>'s this? ____   a. No, it isn't.

2. ____ this your digital camera? ____   b. Yes, he does.

3. ____ are your books? ____   c. They're on the chair.

4. ____ these your headphones? ____   d. It's an electronic dictionary.

5. What are ____? ____   e. Yes, they are.

6. Does he have ____ video game system? ____ f. They're speakers.

Check your English

Unit 4

A Vocabulary

What are they doing? Write the verb.

1. <u>exercise</u>   2. _____   3. _____   4. _____

5. _____   6. _____   7. _____   8. _____

B Grammar

Match the questions with the answers.

1. What's Susan reading? ___

2. Are you watching TV? ___

3. What's Ron doing? ___

4. Are Tim and Ed cooking dinner? ___

5. Where are you? ___

6. Is Bill taking a shower? ___

7. Is Linda at work? ___

8. Are you studying? ___

a. No, she's not. She's at home.

b. He's studying Chinese.

c. No, I'm not. I'm watching a DVD.

d. No, they aren't. They're studying.

e. She's reading her English book.

f. Yes, we're studying English.

g. I'm at school.

h. No, he's not. He's exercising.

Check your English

Unit 5

A   Vocabulary

Read the clues. Write the words.

Across

1. Apples are my favorite ___.

3. She doesn't drink much ___.

4. I like to eat ___ and cheese.

5. We eat ___ at the movies.

8. That Italian restaurant has good ___.

Down

2. I drink a lot of ___.

3. This chocolate ___ is delicious!

4. British people eat a lot of ___.

5. I want some ice cream on my ___.

6. Do you want some potato ___?

7. Do you want tomatoes in your ___?

B   Grammar

Circle the correct words.

1. **A:** How <u>much / many</u> coffee do you drink?

   B: <u>A lot / Much / Many</u>. I really like coffee.

2. My mother <u>cook / cooks</u> dinner every day.

3. My father <u>doesn't / don't</u> like steak.

4. Do you <u>eat / eats</u> Japanese food?

5. Marta likes french fries, but I <u>do / don't</u>.

Check your English

Unit 6

A   Vocabulary

Write the correct word under each picture.

balcony   bathroom   bed   kitchen
lamp   sofa   stairs   yard

1. _____

2. _____

3. _____

4. _____

5. _____

6. _____

7. _____

8. _____

B   Grammar

Put the words in order to make sentences.

1. are   chair   under   the   books   the

   <u>The books are under the chair</u> _____.

2. aren't   plants   room   the   in   any   there

   _____.

3. are   headphones   of   on   the   the   top   TV

   _____.

4. lamp   armchair the   behind   no   is   there

   _____.

Check your English

Unit 7

A   Vocabulary

Read the sentences. Complete the words.

1. You play it with a ball and bat.   It's b a s e b a l l.

2. You can watch this in a theater.   It's a m _ _ _ e.

3. You can work out at this place.   It's a _ y _.

4. People go swimming at this place.   It's a _ e _ c _.

5. Some people do this on weekends.   They _ a _ _ u _.

6. People do this in stores.   They go _ h _ _ p _ _ _ _.

7. We can do this to music.   We d _ _ _ e.

8. People do this with a camera.   They take _ h _ _ _ s.

9. It is a winter sport.   It's _ _ _ w _ _ a _ d _ _ g.

10. You can do this on a computer.   Surf the I _ t _ r _ _ t.

B   Grammar

Complete the questions.

1. A: __What do you do on__ weekends?   B: I play sports.

2. A: _____ you play with?   B: Some friends from work.

3. A: _____ speak English?   B: Yes, she can.

4. A: _____ work out alone?   B: No, I don't.

5. A: _____ ?   B: Yes, I love to go snowboarding.

6. A: _____ read?   B: She usually reads in bed.

7. A: _____ go shopping?   B: I can go on Friday.

8. A: _____ go dancing?   B: He goes dancing on Saturday nights.

9. A: _____ do you eat out?   B: Once or twice a week.

10. A: _____ you play tennis? B: In the park.

Check your English _____

Unit 8

A Vocabulary

Complete the sentences. Use the words below. Use each word only once.

celebrate   vacation   away   graduate
museum   move   rent   stay home

1. People get a diploma when they _____ from high school.

2. There are some wonderful paintings in that _____.

3. My parents are going to _____ to a new house next month.

4. Are you going to have a party to _____ your birthday?

5. You can _____ DVDs in a video store.

6. I'm going to _____ and watch TV tonight.

7. Are you going to go _____ next weekend?

8. When are they going to take a _____?

B Grammar

Match the questions with the answers.

1. Are you going to work this weekend? ___   a. In their apartment.

2. What are you going to do tonight? ___   b. My uncle.

3. Is Hiro going to cook dinner? ___   c. Five days.

4. Where are they going to have the party? ___   d. No, I'm not.

5. When is Alice going to move? ___   e. Next month.

6. Who are you going to play golf with? ___   f. I'm going to study for an exam.

7. Are they going to graduate soon? ___   g. Yes, they are.

8. How long are you going to be in Hong Kong? ___   h. Yes, he is. He's going to make spaghetti.

Check your English

Unit 9

A Vocabulary

What kinds of movies or TV programs are these? Use the words below.

news   comedy   nature program   horror
sports   romance   science fiction   game show

1. This is a funny movie. _____

2. It tells people about events that happen in the world. _____

3. People answer questions to win money. _____

4. It's usually about travel in space. _____

5. It's a scary story, like *Dracula*. _____

6. A man and a woman fall in love. _____

7. It's the World Cup Final. _____

8. It's about animals or plants. _____

B Grammar

Put the words in order to make questions.

1. program   your   what   is   TV   favorite

   What is your favorite TV program? _____?

2. do   movies   why   horror   like   you

   _____?

3. do   game   shows   watch   often   how   you

   _____?

4. your   actor   is   favorite   who

   _____?

5. you   of   what   don't   kind   programs   like   TV

   _____?

6. ever   do   shows   TV   reality   watch   on   you

   _____?

Check your English _____

Unit 10

A Vocabulary

Complete the sentences. Use the words below.

cold   cough syrup   exercise   aspirin
flu   stomachache   terrible   terrific

1. If you have a cough, you can take some _____.

2. She is going to see the doctor because she has the _____.

3. A pain in your stomach is a _____.

4. He has a sore throat and a cough. He has a bad _____.

5. He was sick, but now he feels _____.

6. She's taking some _____ because she has a headache.

7. I'm healthy because I _____ every day.

8. She doesn't feel well. She feels _____.

B Grammar

Complete the conversation. Use the words below.

don't   feel   fever   get   go   have   take   awful

Doctor: How do you _____ today?

Patient: I feel _____.

Doctor: What's the matter?

Patient: I _____ a really bad headache.

Doctor: Do you have a _____ ?

Patient: Yes, and I'm very tired.

Doctor: Maybe you have the flu. _____ home and _____ some rest.
_____ these pills. And _____ go to work.

Check your English

Unit 11

A   Vocabulary

Read the story. Fill in the missing words.

grew up   graduated   moved   took a trip
was born   entered   studied

Tracy Hong __was born__ in Taichung, Taiwan. Her family _____
  1   2

to Los Angeles, California, when she was three. She _____ in
                                                        3

California. She _____ college when she was 18. She _____
                    4   5

French in college. She _____ from college in 2005. The next year
                          6

she _____ to France.
        7

B   Grammar

Read the sentences. Write the correct form of the verbs in parentheses.

Akira and Ben __took__ (take) a trip to San Francisco. They _____ (arrive)

in the city on Friday. They _____ (be) very excited. They _____ (stay)

for the weekend. They _____ (have) a great time. They _____ (eat)

Chinese food in Chinatown. They _____ (attend) a basketball game,

and they _____ (buy) some souvenirs. They _____ (feel) very tired

when they _____ (come) home.

Check your English

Unit 12

A Vocabulary

Write the correct phrase under each picture.

| taking an exam | doing homework | cleaning the apartment | baby-sitting |
| fixing a bicycle | doing the laundry | going to bed early | going to class |

1. _____

2. _____

3. _____

4. _____

5. _____

6. _____

7. _____

8. _____

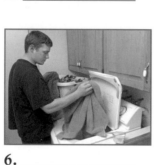

B Grammar

Complete the conversations. Circle the correct words.

Conversation A

A: Could / Would I please speak to Amy?

B: She's at the library. Can / Do you want to leave a message?

A: Yes, please. Ask she / her to call Bill at work.

B: Does she / her have the phone number?

A: Yes, she has it / him.

Conversation B

A: Do you want / like to see a movie tonight?

B: I'd like / want to, but I can't. I have / have to work late.

A: Well, would / do you like to go to the movies with me tomorrow night?

B: Sure, I'd love / I love to!

Key vocabulary

Here is a list of most of the new words in *Talk Time 1*.

adj = adjective
adv = adverb
conj = conjunction
det = determiner
n = noun
prep = preposition
pron = pronoun
v = verb

Unit 1

address   *n*
American   *n*
apartment number   *n*
aren't   *v*
artist   *n*
athlete   *n*
Australia   *n*
Australian   *n*

be   *v*
Brazil   *n*
Brazilian   *n*
British   *n*
business person   *n*

China   *n*
Chinese   *n*
class   *n*
country   *n*

e-mail address   *n*

first name   *n*
from   *prep*

he   *pron*
hello
her   *adj, pron*
hi
his   *adj, pron*
How about you?

I   *pron*
India   *n*
Indian   *n*
it   *pron*

Japan   *n*
Japanese   *n*

Korea   *n*
Korean   *n*

last name   *n*

meet   *v*
movie star   *n*

my   *adj*
name   *n*
nationality   *n*
Nice to meet you.
nickname   *n*
no

OK

people   *n*
phone number   *n*
politician   *n*

she   *pron*
singer   *n*
student   *n*

telephone number   *n*
they   *pron*

the U.K.   *n*
the U.S.A.   *n*

what/what's   *pron*
we   *pron*
where   *adv*
who/who's   *pron*

yes
you   *pron*
your   *pron*

Unit 2

age   *n*
aunt   *n*
average height/
weight   *adj*

beautiful   *adj*
blond   *adj*
blue   *adj*
brother   *n*
brown   *adj*

children   *n*
cousin   *n*
curly   *adj*

cute   *adj*
dark   *adj*
daughter   *n*
doesn't   *v*
don't   *v*

eyes   *n*

family   *n*
father   *n*

good-looking   *adj*
grandchildren   *n*
granddaughter   *n*
grandfather   *n*
grandmother   *n*
grandparents   *n*
grandson   *n*

hair   *n*
handsome   *adj*
have   *v*
heavy   *adj*
height   *n*
husband   *n*

in his (twenties)   *adj*

long   *adj*

married   *adj*
middle-aged   *adj*
mother   *n*

nephew   *n*
nice   *adj*
niece   *n*

old   *adj*

parents   *n*
pretty   *adj*

relationship   *n*

short   *adj*
single   *adj*
sister   *n*
son   *n*
straight   *adj*

tall *adj*
that/that's *pron*
thin *adj*

uncle *n*

weight *n*
who/who's *pron*
wife *n*

young *adj*

Unit 3

a/an *det*

board *n*
book *n*
bookbag *n*
boom box *n*
bulletin board *n*

camcorder *n*
camera *n*
CD player *n*
cell phone *n*
chair *n*
classroom *n*
clock *n*

desk *n*
digital camera *n*
doesn't *v*
DVD player *n*

electronic dictionary *n*
electronics *n*
eraser *n*

floor *n*

headphones *n*

karaoke machine *n*

laptop *n*
like *v*

map *n*
May I help you?
MP3 player *n*

notebook *n*

on *prep*

pen *n*
pencil *n*

ruler *n*

speaker *n*

table *n*
television/TV *n*
thanks a lot
that *pron*
these *pron*
this *pron*
those *pron*

video game system *n*

wall *n*
wastebasket *n*

Unit 4

activity *n*
at *prep*

cooking *v*

dinner *n*
doing *v*
drinking *v*
driving *v*

eating *v*
everyday *adj*
exercising *v*

home *n*

in *prep*

not *adv*
nothing much (*informal*)

playing the piano *v*

reading *v*

school *n*
shopping *v*

singing *v*
sleeping *v*
store *n*
street *n*
studying *v*

taking a shower *v*
talking on the phone *v*
theater *n*

washing dishes *v*
work *n*

Unit 5

a lot (of)
appetizer *n*
apple *n*

beverage *n*
broiled *adj*
but *conj*

cake *n*
carrot *n*
chicken *n*
chocolate *n*
coffee *n*
cookie *n*

dessert *n*
do/don't/doesn't *v*
drink *n*

eat *v*
either *adv*
every *adv*

food *n*
fish *n*
french fries *n*
fried *adj*
fruit *n*

good *adj*
great *adj*
Greek salad *n*
green salad *n*

house salad *n*

ice cream *n*

Italian *adj*

know *v*

let's go *v*

like *v*

love *v*

main course *n*

many *pron*

meat *n*

mineral water *n*

mixed *adj*

mousse *n*

much *pron*

nut *n*

pie *n*

popcorn *n*

potato chip *n*

pretzels *n*

restaurant *n*

rice cake *n*

roast *adj*

sauce *n*

snack *n*

soda *n*

some *pron*

soup *n*

spaghetti *n*

steak *n*

tea *n*

tomato *n*

vegetable *n*

yeah (*informal*)

Unit 6

apartment *n*

armchair *n*

balcony *n*

bathroom *n*

bed *n*

bedroom *n*

behind *prep*

between *prep*

big *adj*

bookcase *n*

closet *n*

coffee table *n*

dining room *n*

dresser *n*

first/second floor *n*

garage *n*

hall *n*

house *n*

housing *n*

in front of *prep*

kitchen *n*

lamp *n*

living room *n*

look for *v*

next to *prep*

on top of *prep*

picture *n*

plant *n*

room *n*

sofa *n*

stairs *n*

swimming pool *n*

terrace *n*

there are *v*

there is/there's *v*

under *prep*

window *n*

yard *n*

Unit 7

anywhere *adv*

baseball *n*

basketball *n*

can *v*

can not *v*

can't *v*

cannot *v*

cycling *n*

dance *v*

department store *n*

eat out *v*

every day *adv*

free time *n*

go dancing *v*

go shopping *v*

go to the beach *v*

go to the movies *v*

golf *n*

how often?

ice-skating *n*

judo *n*

just *adv*

listen to music *v*

never *adv*

oh

once *adv*

paint *v*

play *v*

play cards *v*

popular *adj*

skiing *n*

snowboarding *n*

soccer *n*

sports *n*

swimming *n*

take photos *v*

tennis   *n*
times a week/month   *adv*
to do   *v*
twice   *adv*

volleyball   *n*

watch TV   *v*
What about you?
windsurfing   *n*
winter   *n*
with   *prep*
work out at a gym   *v*

Unit 8

be born   *v*
boring   *adj*

celebrate a birthday   *v*

date a boyfriend/girlfriend   *v*

excited   *adj*
event   *n*

fabulous   *adj*
fall in love   *v*
few   *pron*

get a job   *v*
go away   *v*
go to college   *v*
going to   *v*
graduate   *v*

hour   *n*
how long?

interesting   *adj*

later   *adv*
library   *n*
life   *n*

meet friends   *v*
move   *v*

plans   *n*

rent a DVD   *v*

rent an apartment   *v*
someday   *adv*
soon   *adv*
sounds like   *v*
spend time with family   *v*
start school   *v*
stay   *v*
stay home   *v*
study for an exam   *v*

take a vacation   *v*
today   *adv*
tonight   *adv*
travel   *v*

visit a museum   *v*

week   *n*
when   *adv*
work   *v*
wow

year   *n*

Unit 9

action   *adj*
actor   *n*
actress   *n*
always   *adv*
animated   *adj*

can't stand   *v*
cartoon   *n*
children's program   *n*
comedy   *n, adj*

dislike   *v*
drama   *n*

fantasy   *n, adj*
favorite   *adj*

game show   *n*
get up   *v*

hardly ever   *adv*
horror   *adj*

kind   *n*

movie   *n*

nature program   *n*
news   *n*
night (at night)   *n*

often   *adv*

program   *n*

reality show   *n*
romance   *n, adj*

science-fiction   *n, adj*
sitcom   *n*
soap opera   *n*
sometimes   *adv*
surprising   *adj*

talk show   *n*

usually   *adv*

why?

Unit 10

aspirin   *n*
awful   *adj*

backache   *n*
bath   *n*
better   *adj*

cold (a cold)   *n*
cough   *n*
cough syrup   *n*

dentist   *n*
doctor   *n*
don't worry   *v*

earache   *n*

feel   *v*
fever   *n*
fine   *adj*
flu   *n*

get some exercise   *v*

hard   *adv*
headache   *n*
hope   *v*
hot   *adj*

I'm afraid...   (*idiom*)

not so good (*informal*)

problem   *n*

relax   *v*

see   *v*
sick   *adj*
sore throat   *n*
sorry to hear that
stay in bed   *v*
stomachache   *n*

terrible   *adj*
terrific   *adj*
that's too bad (*informal*)
tired   *adj*
toothache   *n*

what's the matter?
what's wrong?

Unit 11

ago   *adv*
arrived   *v*
ate in restaurants   *v*
attended   *v*

best friend   *n*
bought   *v*

came   *v*

did/didn't   *v*

enjoy   *v*

a good time   *n*
graduated   *v*
grew up   *v*

had   *v*
high school   *n*

in love   *n*

late   *adv*

moved   *v*

no kidding (*informal*)

problem   *n*

remember   *v*
rented a car   *v*

slept   *v*
souvenir   *n*
studied maps   *v*
sure (= *yes*)

took *v*
took pictures   *v*

trip   *n*

visited   *v*

was/wasn't   *v*
went   *v*
were/weren't   *v*

Unit 12

after   *adv*
answering machine   *n*

baby-sit   *v*
beep   *n*

call   *v*
can   *v*
clean   *v*
come to the phone   *v*
come over   *v*
could   *v*

early   *adv*

fix a bicycle   *v*

go to bed   *v*
go to class   *v*
good-bye/bye

have to   *v*

her   *pron*
him   *pron*
homework   *n*

I'd   *v*
I'm sorry.
introduce yourself   *v*
it *pron*

laundry   *n*
leave a message   *v*
like to   *v*
listen   *v*

make a phone call   *v*
me   *pron*
message   *n*
most   *adv*

need to   *v*
now   *adv*

right (= *correct*)   *adv*

right now   *adv*

speak   *v*

take a message   *v*
take an exam   *v*
text message   *n*
tell   *v*
them   *pron*
thing   *n*

us   *pron*

want to   *v*
would (would you?)   *v*